HALFWAY TO HEAVEN

The author in middle age

RUPERT HART-DAVIS

Halfway to Heaven

CONCLUDING MEMOIRS OF A LITERARY LIFE

When I have fears that I may cease to be
Before my pen has glean'd my teeming brain
KEATS

Look thy last on all things lovely,
Every hour – let no night
Seal thy sense in deathly slumber
Till to delight
Thou hast paid thy utmost blessing;
Since that all things thou wouldst praise
Beauty took from those who loved them
In other days.
DE LA MARE

SUTTON PUBLISHING

First published in the United Kingdom in 1998 by
Sutton Publishing Limited · Phoenix Mill
Thrupp · Stroud · Gloucestershire · GL5 2BU

British Library Cataloguing in Publication Data
A catalogue record for this book is available from the British Library.

ISBN 0-7509-1837-3

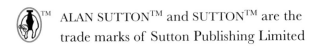
ALAN SUTTON™ and SUTTON™ are the
trade marks of Sutton Publishing Limited

Typeset in 10/15.5 pt New Baskerville.
Typesetting and origination by
Sutton Publishing Limited.
Printed in Great Britain by
WBC Ltd, Bridgend.

To My Beloved Junie

For more than thirty years, my sweet,
You've made my happiness,
And every problem that you meet
You solve with great finesse.

Your beauty grows with every day,
As does your loving care.
You cosset me in every way
And everything you share.

Where can age and beauty meet?
In your lovely face, my sweet.
Large brown eyes and silver curls
Put you above all other girls.

You guard me on the telephone.
Without you I'd have perished long ago.
I hate the thought of you left all alone
For I do love you so.

BOOKS BY RUPERT HART-DAVIS

Hugh Walpole, a biography 1952
The Lyttelton Hart-Davis Letters, 6 vols 1978–84
The Arms of Time, a memoir 1979
A Beggar in Purple, a commonplace book 1983
The Power of Chance, a table of memory 1991
Praise from the Past, tributes to writers 1996

BOOKS COMPILED, EDITED AND INTRODUCED BY RUPERT HART-DAVIS

The Second Omnibus Book (Heinemann) 1930
Then and Now (Cape) 1935
The Essential Neville Cardus (Cape) 1949
Cricket All His Life by E.V. Lucas (RHD Ltd) 1950
All in Due Time by Humphry House (RHD Ltd) 1955
George Moore: Letters to Lady Cunard 1895–1933 (RHD Ltd) 1957
The Letters of Oscar Wilde (RHD Ltd) 1962
Max Beerbohm: Letters to Reggie Turner (RHD Ltd) 1964
More Theatres by Max Beerbohm (RHD Ltd) 1969
Last Theatres by Max Beerbohm (RHD Ltd) 1970
A Peep into the Past by Max Beerbohm (Heinemann) 1972
A Catalogue of the Caricatures of Max Beerbohm (Macmillan) 1972
The Autobiography of Arthur Ransome (Cape) 1976
Electric Delights by William Plomer (Cape) 1978
Selected Letters of Oscar Wilde (Oxford) 1979
Two Men of Letters (Michael Joseph) 1979
Siegfried Sassoon: Diaries 1920–1922 3 vols. (Faber) 1981–85
War Poems of Siegfried Sassoon (Faber) 1983
More Letters of Oscar Wilde (Murray) 1985
Siegfried Sassoon: Letters to Max Beerbohm (Faber) 1986
Letters of Max Beerbohm (Murray) 1986

CONTENTS

ILLUSTRATIONS

INTRODUCTION

This book is the last of a trilogy covering the whole of my long life. Its first predecessor was *The Arms of Time* (1979) which begins with the birth of my great-great-great-grandmother Mrs Jordan, the mistress of William IV, in 1761 and so on to the birth in 1886 of my beloved mother, who died in 1929 when I was nineteen and my sister Deirdre was seventeen.

Its successor was *The Power of Chance* (1991) in which, after two miserable terms at Balliol College, Oxford, I became an acting student at the Old Vic, and so heard and learnt a great deal of Shakespeare. I fell in love with and married the actress Peggy Ashcroft, but soon realised that I would never become a leading actor and our marriage broke up.

I had always been fascinated by books and managed to get a job as office boy in the publishing firm of William Heinemann Ltd. I stayed there for two years and then became the operative secretary of the Book Society for a year; then I moved on to be the junior director of Jonathan Cape Ltd.

In 1933 I married Comfort Borden Turner, the daughter of the novelist Mary Borden, who presented me with two sons and a daughter. When the war started Comfort's wealthy aunt in America begged me to send her and the children over to get them out of the war area. Reluctantly I did this and enlisted as a private soldier in the Coldstream Guards, where I served for the duration of the war.

This book contains an account of my main doings in the next fifty years, except for the years 1955–62 when everything I did was described in my letters to George Lyttelton, which were published in six volumes in *The Lyttelton Hart-Davis Letters*.

I must thank my old publishing colleagues, Teddy Young, Harry Townshend, Guy Fisher and Richard Garnett for vetting the typescript of this book, and I am doubly grateful to Richard for permission to print the letter from his father David and for his amazing tribute on my ninetieth birthday.

Rupert Hart-Davis
Marske-in-Swaledale
March 1998

PART ONE: A FIRM IS BORN

Of making books there is no end,
And much study is a weariness of the flesh.
ECCLESIASTES

The object of writing is to enable the reader
to enjoy life or better to endure it.
DR JOHNSON

[1]

I WAS THIRTY-EIGHT when I was demobilised from the Army on 29 October 1945. The theatre and the army were adventures of the past, and there remained only the book-trade. My first indebtedness was to Jonathan Cape Ltd, of which I had been a director since 1933. When I enlisted in 1940 my salary was £900 a year, and they had paid me half that amount in each of my five military years. I was not eager to return there because I saw little hope of financial or other promotion. So, in a letter to Jonathan and Bob Howard I suggested three subjects which we might discuss when we met.

1) That my salary should be increased to £1,800 to keep pace with the cost of living.
2) That I should be allowed to buy shares in the company, if I ever had the money. (They had long ago given me a thousand notional shares of one pound each.)
3) That the managing director's annual bonus should be paid in an agreed ratio. (In one year in the late 1930s the two of them shared £10,000, while I was given £400.) I suggested 40 per cent to each of them and 20 per cent to me.

Jonathan's reply was long, cold and windy, as his letters often were, and in it he said that my 'unreasonable proposals' did not offer any basis for discussion. I answered as follows:

1 November 1945   *Bromsden Farm, Henley-on-Thames, Oxon*

My dear Jonathan,

How sad that it should come to this. I had hoped that you would be sufficiently interested in my return to advance an inch or two to meet my suggestions, but your letter is so wholly intransigent that there seems nothing more to be said. I worked for you for seven years before the war, and if the best testimonial you can give me is 'We would not say that you had nothing to do with [the firm's] progress', I certainly look like making more progress elsewhere. I could give you a list of books and authors that I brought you, but there seems little point.[1] You have spoken in no uncertain manner, and it only remains for me to make graceful – and regretful – adieux.

Your ever, R.

[2]

The seed of Rupert Hart-Davis Ltd had been sown four years earlier, in this letter from David Garnett. I had first met him with his father Edward (E.G.) who always called him David. I did the same, though almost all his family and friends called him Bunny.

10 February 1941   *Claverham Farm, Berwick, Polegate, Sussex*

My dear Rupert,

Thank goodness you are alive. When I heard that idiot broadcast about making men march 65 miles a day with full packs, I thought

---

1 I could have cited Duff Cooper, Peter Fleming, Robert Frost, Neville Cardus, William Plomer, Cecil Day Lewis, Beachcomber, Edmund Blunden, J. Maclaren Ross and Lord Wavell, as well as a long list of authors brought to the firm by Peter and William.

of you and your knee and wondered whether we should have nothing but an army of cripples to face the Germans when they land. You have tried to do what T.E. did without his toughness. You remember Uxbridge nearly killed him.[1] It's all very well laying down your life for your country – but to lay it down for a drill instructor is not sweet however decorous – and decorum is not enough, as Nurse Cavell ought to have said.

I suppose if they don't kill you, or cripple you, you will remain in the army till after the war. Have you thought of what you'll do then? I ask because your letter has suddenly put into my head that you should set up on your own account as a publisher, and that I might conceivably join you if I have any capital at that time. I may have.

After the war there will be a burst of intellectual curiosity of all kinds. Thousands of soldiers will feel they have missed a lot and will turn eagerly to reading books, and some of them to writing them. We shall want to know about Europe too and shall hear what the French have to say – and dare I say it – the Dutch, Danes, Poles, Belgians and all the different brands of German.

I am afraid such words will sound almost as though E.G. were speaking from the grave. But if my suggestion makes you smile so much the better.

I realise that though you can say NO in emphatic terms, you can't possibly say yes. So tuck the idea away. Of course I don't really know that I want to be a publisher: what I do know is that I don't want to be a journalist and indeed shall not be one. I am now writing my elementary book about the Air War and hope to get it done by the early summer – or to publish then. I am rather in the position of Sterne who reflected after writing *Tristram Shandy* for a year that he was living 365 times as fast as he wrote his autobiography. But maybe I shall catch up.

Yours ever DAVID

---

1 See *The Mint* by T.E. Lawrence, in which he recounts his experiences as an aircraftsman in the Royal Air Force.

To which I replied:

15 February 1941   *as from Bromsden Farm, Henley-on-Thames, Oxon*

My dear David,

Your most delightful letter was forwarded to me in the Cotswolds, where I am spending a few days with my father-in-law. Far from making me smile, your publishing suggestion has stimulated and excited me – and if your prognostications of the post-war situation bear echoes of E.G.'s voice, what could be more welcome? To begin with, wash out that capital NO. Even if it comes to nix, let's discuss it a bit before we tuck it away. I must confess that the thought of taking up the same impotent position [with Cape] and keeping the place warm for our friends' sons, fills me with *une immense fatigue*. On the other hand I might conceivably be in a strong position just after the war. Jonathan is reported to have announced his forthcoming retirement.[1] If this really takes place, the sons will not be old enough to come in, and, temporarily at any rate, I might hold a pistol at all heads. But that is supposition. How I wish we could talk it all over, but I see no chance at present. We should have tremendous fun with our publishing, but should we make a living? I think it possible.

Between us, our literary 'connection' is considerable, and we have the advantage (or, remembering No. 30,[2] is it a disadvantage?) of being really interested in books. I suppose we should need a sort of younger Bob to cope with a lot of Bobbish detail? You say you may have some capital. Just now I have none, but if my Highgate house remains unbombed and I sell it well, after the war, and if I left J.C. and cashed in on the 1,000 shares they gave me, I might raise £3,000 or even £4,000. Goodness knows how much we'd want. J.C. started with £10,000, I believe, but only half of that was

1 In fact he never retired, but struggled on, through age and illness, until he died in 1960, aged eighty.
2 Cape's office at 30 Bedford Square, where Bob Howard was in charge of all book production, dealing with printers and binders, etc.

ever needed. Would it be suicidal to start a business in some town other than London – say Oxford? I do hate having to go to London every day, don't you? This idea of yours is the first thing that has excited me for months and months. Write again and keep it going. I return to Bromsden Farm on Monday – and on Thursday I go to Sandhurst (Camberley) for three months. Then, if alive, I become an officer. Will send you the Sandhurst address as soon as I know it.

Love RUPERT

P.S. Keep the publishing notion under your hat.

Now, in 1945, remembering this exchange, I got in touch with David. We met and discussed the publishing idea, of which he was still much in favour. Seeking a production manager I wrote to Teddy Young, whom I had known before the war when he was working for World Books. Earlier he had been in at the birth of Penguin Books and drew the original penguin which became their trademark. During the war he served as a submariner, escaped from a submarine which had been sunk after a collision with a British trawler, and later became the first Royal Naval Volunteer Reserve officer to command his own submarine. He was awarded a DSO for gallantry, as well as a DSC and bar.[1]

I told him of my and David's ideas and asked whether he would like to join us. On 29 December 1945 he answered from his home at Redhill, saying that he had gone back to World Books, but was feeling restless, and had toyed with the idea of starting on his own, though he had so far failed to raise enough capital.

On 16 January 1946 he came up to London and we lunched at the Guards' Club, finding that our ideas fitted together nicely. Thereafter he wrote me two long, enthusiastic and businesslike letters. On 4 February I spent a night with him and his wife at Redhill, and soon after that introduced him to David. They got on very well, so now all we needed were an office, money, and paper.

---

1 We published his excellent book *One of Our Submarines* in 1952.

[3]

The office problem was quickly solved by the power of chance. My sister Deirdre's and my friend Mary Booker had just rented a house, 53 Connaught Street, near Marble Arch. She didn't need the ground floor and basement, so let them to us at a tiny rent. The ground floor consisted of a small shop, from which a steep and narrow staircase descended to the basement, which covered the whole area of the house. Down there a small room became my office, a large room at the back Teddy's (David came to the office only occasionally) and between were packing-benches and shelves for books.

Inside the main front door of the house was a long passage leading to the back of the house, at the end of which was a snug little room with its own bathroom and WC. It was wonderfully quiet and peaceful, backing over a high wall on to the Archery Ground.

We moved into the offices in January 1946. David bought most of the desks, chairs and other furniture that we needed at country sales. At a minor airfield he bought us a small van, just right for London traffic.

Now for money. Long ago Jonathan Cape had given me a thousand one-pound shares in the company, but when I suggested buying a few more shares he told me they were now worth three pounds each. Accordingly I wrote to him, saying that money would now be more useful to me than shares, asking him if he would like to have my shares back and reminding him of the enhanced value he had put on them. He immediately sent me a cheque for £3,000 and I returned the share certificate. Altogether we scrambled together £15,000, helped by generous author-friends such as Arthur Ransome, Geoffrey Keynes and Eric Linklater. We realised that we couldn't possibly publish our first books until 1947, and meanwhile Teddy and I must have something to live on. So we allotted each other £800 for the first year, out of our capital.

Then came the hideous problem of paper. It was strictly rationed and each firm was allowed a percentage of what it had used in 1938. If a firm didn't exist then it got nothing. But there was a very modest ex-serviceman's ration, which would be enough for one medium-sized book. Teddy applied for his quota and got it, but when I wrote to the Board of Trade explaining that I too was an ex-serviceman, they said no, only one such quota for each firm.

Then a delightful Glasgow bookseller called Alan Jackson, whom I had known before the war, wrote to say that, since he had done a little publishing in the pre-war years, he now had a paper quota which he didn't need and would gladly sell to me at cost price. I gratefully accepted his generous offer.

Having joined the Publishers' Association I attended their Annual General Meeting and made a powerful speech on behalf of small new firms like my own. This had two results: the President of the PA, a very nice man called B.W. Fagan, MC, who was head of Edward Arnold Ltd, took me to the Board of Trade, where we persuaded them to double the ex-serviceman's quota. The result was amusing. I and Dennis Cohen, a great friend who had founded the Cresset Press, were elected to the Council of the PA to represent small publishers. At our first meeting three-quarters of the time was spent discussing Visual Aids. We had no idea what these were, but missed the moment of asking, and it wasn't till our fourth meeting that we got the answer.

At the end of our first meeting there was a discussion about a defaulting bookseller, at the end of which Daniel Macmillan, a twitchy neurotic man, said in a loud voice: 'And I don't mind telling you that the fellow's real name was COHEN.' There was an appalled silence until Dennis laughed. I don't think Dan ever realised his terrible gaffe.

[4]

At the beginning of 1946 I spent the best part of a week with my bookseller friend Dudley Massey in Christie's basement, sorting out lots of the fourth section of the sale of Hugh Walpole's library. Ever since Hugh's death in 1941 I had been trying to think of a suitable person to write his life. I made a list of all his surviving friends, but none of them would do, for it was a tricky job. Hugh was wholly homosexual, but such facts were not publicly exposed in those days, and his unmarried sister and brother would have been horrified by any such disclosure. What was needed was a full and faithful life written by someone who was fond of him which would make Hugh's sexual predilections obvious to homosexuals, while old ladies who had never heard of homosexuality could happily enjoy the book.

I went to see Hugh's publisher Harold Macmillan, now temporarily out of office during the Labour government. I explained my difficulty, and made the outrageous suggestion that I should have a go at the book myself. He said he thought that an excellent idea and promised to send me a contract immediately. I still have it, dated 8 January 1946 and signed by the future Prime Minister.

I left his presence with my morale sky-high. I had never before put together more than 1,500 consecutive words, but somehow, during almost seven years of work in all my spare time, I produced a volume of 180,000 words (many of them quotations from letters, diaries and books) which was published by Macmillan in March 1952, and is still (in 1998) in print as a paperback.

[5]

Now, with an office, some money, an enlarged ex-serviceman's paper ration, and the black market, we were ready to start. We dared not begin with a living author, for the wartime boom in bookselling was still in force, and if the first edition of a book was sold out quickly we would have no paper for a reprint, and the author would surely leave us. So we decided to start with books by dead authors. David and I were both admirers of Henry James, whose books were all out of print, but before we began his resurrection I sent a spy round to Macmillan's, who had published all James's later work. A packer there told the spy: ''Enry James? We've been packin' parcels with the sheets of 'Enry James for donkey's years.'

PUBLICATIONS FOR THE YEAR

HENRY JAMES

* FOURTEEN STORIES
Selected, with an Introduction, by
DAVID GARNETT
Large Crown 8vo. 473 pp. *15s net*
THE FOLLOWING NOVELS BY HENRY JAMES WILL
SHORTLY BE PUBLISHED, UNIFORM WITH THE
ABOVE:

THE OTHER HOUSE 256 pp. *8s 6d net*
THE TRAGIC MUSE 640 pp. *15s net*

JOSHUA SLOCUM

SAILING ALONE AROUND THE WORLD
and
VOYAGE OF THE LIBERDADE
(never before published in Great Britain)
together in one volume
with an introduction by ARTHUR RANSOME
Over 30 illustrations, including a new folding chart.
Crown 8vo. 8s 6d net

RUPERT BROOKE

*DEMOCRACY AND THE ARTS
A hitherto unpublished Essay by RUPERT
BROOKE, with an introduction by GEOFFREY
KEYNES, and a new portrait frontispiece.
Large Crown 8vo. 6s net
There are still a few copies left of the Limited
Edition on part-rag paper, quarter-bound in real
niger; at 31s 6d net

THE COMPLETE NOVELS OF PEACOCK

IN ONE VOLUME
HEADLONG HALL | MELINCOURT
MAID MARIAN | CROTCHET CASTLE
NIGHTMARE ABBEY | GRYLL GRANGE
THE MISFORTUNES OF ELPHIN
Large Crown 8vo. Over 1,000 pages. 10s 6d net

ERIC LINKLATER

SEALSKIN TROUSERS
AND OTHER STORIES
with wood engravings by JOAN HASSALL
Large Crown 8vo. 7s 6d net

THE LIFE OF WILLIAM BLAKE

BY MONA WILSON
Originally issued by the Nonesuch Press in a
limited edition, this standard life of Blake will
now be made available to a wider public.
Demy 8vo. Illustrated. 18s net

DAVID GARNETT

A NEW VOLUME OF STORIES
(TITLE TO BE ANNOUNCED LATER)
Large Crown 8vo. 8s 6d net

G. M. YOUNG

A NEW VOLUME OF ESSAYS
(TITLE TO BE ANNOUNCED LATER)
Large Crown 8vo. 8s. 6d. net

* Already published. Other publication dates are not yet fixed. Prices subject to alteration.

RUPERT HART-DAVIS
53 CONNAUGHT STREET LONDON W.2 (PADDINGTON 5909)

Our first advertisement

Thus reassured, David set out on the selection of what became *Fourteen Stories by Henry James*, which, though dated 1946, was not published until 14 February 1947, along with an unknown undergraduate talk called *Democracy and the Arts* by Rupert Brooke. Both books were praised by reviewers for their content and their appearance.

We had decided that our emblem should be a fox, in memory of David's best-known novel *Lady into Fox*, and Reynolds Stone made a fine compact woodcut of a sitting fox, which appeared on the title-pages of these, our first books, and on a great many others. When I discovered that double-column advertisements in periodicals were charged by the inch, I asked Reynolds if he could produce a running fox, which would be half as expensive. He, bless him, produced one immediately. David's wife Angelica painted a lovely signboard for us. It had a fox on each side with the firm's name above. We fixed it just above the window of the office, so that whichever way people were walking on the pavement they couldn't miss it.

Eric Linklater, who had already contributed £1,000 to our original capital, which I'm sure he couldn't afford, now sent me, as he finished writing them, five delightful short stories, which regardless of our fear

Reynolds Stone's fox

Signboard by
Angelica Garnett

of living authors, we published on 24 October 1947 as *Sealskin Trousers*. The book was illustrated, at Eric's suggestion, with exquisite wood-engravings by Joan Hassall, to whose fee Eric insisted on contributing. Her fox on the title-page graced many of our later books. We printed 25,000 copies and sold them all. The first big success in our first year.

At this time it was difficult to find any decent cloth for bindings, and one day when I was looking through a packet of specimens I suddenly turned them over and discovered that the back of one of

Joan Hassall's fox

them was an attractive light blue. We bound Eric's book in it, and were congratulated on finding such distinguished *buckram*. To reward Eric for his generosity I had fifty large-paper copies printed on hand-made paper and bound in half-leather, which were signed by him and Joan Hassall. They signed the fifty copies at the binder's. Eric had enjoyed a lavish lunch at the Savile Club, and after he had signed some twenty copies he said: 'I'm getting bored with this. I think I'll sign J.B. Priestley for a bit.' Joan and I coaxed him back to his duty.

One Saturday, when we were immensely busy in the office, Teddy brought a colleague of his at World Books to help us out. She was a young, neat, pretty girl called June Clifford. Some years later, by the power of chance, her fate and mine were to be sealed.

Meanwhile at home my wife Comfort, the mother of my children, was undergoing a complete change of personality. I first noticed it in

1943. We had always planned to have four children, but after Adam was born Comfort said she didn't want any more, and would prefer to have no more love-making. This was a terrible blow to me, but I could only accept it with docility. The loving merriment which little Bridget had remarked on when she came home from America gradually faded and was succeeded by a withdrawn and almost impersonal competence. The laughing, loving girl I had married ten years before was turning into a benevolent automaton. She worked hard in house and garden and looked after the children without emotion like a kind matron in a school. In all the subsequent years I remember no cross word between us.

With hindsight and the knowledge of modern medicine I can trace each symptom of her decline. She was suffering from a rare circulatory disorder which is now known as Huerger's disease, after an American doctor Leo Huerger (1879–1943), who in 1908 wrote the first clear report of the clinical course and pathology of the illness. The only thing he failed to discover was its cause, and it wasn't until some years after his death that the cause was positively identified as heavy smoking.

I imagine that Comfort contracted the habit during the unhappy year (1940–41) which she spent with Bridget and Duff in America. Anyhow the craving continued until her first action on waking in the morning was to light a cigarette and to keep one going all day whatever she was doing: she even smoked in the bath, and her last act at night was to stub out a cigarette before she switched off her bedside light. Goodness knows how many she smoked in a day. She twice tried to give up smoking, but each time became so ill that she returned to the habit.

Gradually she underwent all the symptoms described by Huerger – a tremendously high blood-pressure, for which she had to be rushed to hospital, later hardening of the arteries and gangrene in one leg, which had to be amputated below the knee. She lived on till 1970 and died in a cottage attached to Bridget's farm. One morning she was found dead in bed, with a cigarette in her fingers. Luckily it had gone out.

[6]

Looking for further books to publish, especially short ones, I wrote to Theodora Bosanquet, who had been Henry James's secretary, to ask whether I might reprint (if possible in an extended form) her excellent pamphlet *Henry James at Work*, which had been published by Leonard and Virginia Woolf in 1924. She pleaded her age, her busyness, her disinclination to tinker with something written so long ago, and advised me instead to get in touch with a brilliant young American who had published a thesis in French on Henry James's 'dramatic years'.

Clutching at this straw I despatched a letter to Lt J.L. Edel 02026430, Information Control Div., HQ U.S.F.E.T., APO 757, c/o US Army, little guessing that this would lead to one of the most rewarding and delightful friendships of my life. A few months later I received a cordial answer from 58 West 83rd Street, New York. From it I learned that the writer's first name was Leon and that he was working as a journalist.

One day, when David was staying with me at Bromsden Farm, we agreed that Teddy wasn't very keen on Henry James, and that we must

A visit to Arthur Ransome in the garden of his Hill Top Cottage in the Lakes

Adam, Bridget and Duff at Tenby

try to find a nautical book to please him. David said: 'Round the world voyagers?' I said: 'Captain Cook?' David said: 'Joshua Slocum?', but neither of us knew anything about him. At that moment the telephone rang. It was Arthur Ransome, apologising about something. I said: 'I'll forgive you if you tell me who Joshua Slocum was.' Arthur said: 'He wrote the best small-boat sailing book ever written, and if you reissue it I'll write you an introduction for nothing.' 'Done', said I, and we published the book in April 1948. *Sailing Alone Around the World* received a rapturous press and became Volume One of a series of reprints of similar sailing books which we called The Mariners Library. In the end it contained more than forty volumes, including Ransome's *Racundra's First Cruise*. He also wrote introductions to six other titles.

In the middle of August 1946 we took the children – Bridget (eleven), Duff (ten) and Adam (three) – for a fortnight's holiday at Tenby on the lovely Pembrokeshire coast. We stayed in a boarding house very near the beach, where the children played happily on the sand and splashed about on the edge of the sea.

One evening, as I was walking back from putting the car away, I suddenly came upon what seemed to be a vision – a beautiful woman in the middle of the road with a book in her hand. She came towards me and said: 'I'm sure you don't remember me or know who I am.' For a split second I didn't know, and then in a flash I said: 'Of course I know you. You're Ruth Simon and it's lovely to see you.'

She was staying in a hotel with her children, Jill and Timothy, who were both still at school. I had met her first in 1938 at a cricket match at Ightham in Kent between my Cape eleven and her husband's Curwen Press. After the match the painter Graham Sutherland and his wife, who were living nearby, asked us all in for drinks. Ruth and I sat on a sofa and talked of mutual friends, especially Hamish Miles, who had recently died. I remember driving back to London very fast with a feeling of elation. Comfort and I dined once with the Simons in their house in Downshire Hill, Hampstead, and they dined once with us in our Highgate home. I didn't see her again until she discovered by chance that I was taking my family to Tenby and immediately booked rooms for herself and her children in a hotel there.

Ruth and I walked and talked on the sands every day. She was very interested in my emerging firm, in which Comfort took no interest. On a wet afternoon I took her to the movie *Casablanca* which is as good today as it was fifty years ago. We agreed to meet in London.

[7]

For most of 1946 I had commuted five days a week from Henley to Paddington, but as soon as the snug bedroom behind the office was fully furnished I spent four weekday nights there each week, working on Hugh. Also, whenever possible, Ruth and I had lunch there, usually sandwiches and a bottle of wine from Capri. There,

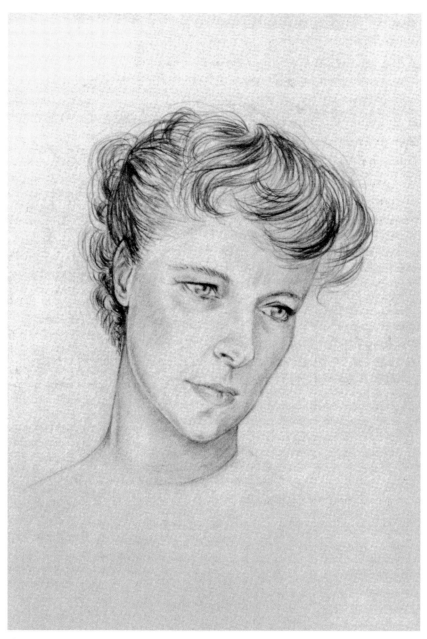

Ruth by Consuelo Haydon

just before Christmas, we were able for the first time to make passionate love. Our sexual affinity was perfect and lasted for twenty years. Neither of us had experienced such complete harmony before.

Ruth, to ease her boredom, had for some time been taking lessons in graphology from a remarkable expert called Mrs Jacoby. Many important businesses refused to take on new recruits until Mrs Jacoby had analysed their character by their handwriting. I gave Ruth a page of one of Hugh Walpole's manuscripts which contained no signs of his identity or occupation. From it Mrs Jacoby made a wonderfully accurate analysis of Hugh's character and profession. I couldn't resist sending Ruth this little poem:

> You thought to study handwriting,
> And I planned to write on Hugh.
> (We planned to decline on intellect,
> So staid, so wise, so circumspect).
> But since love took a hand, my sweet,
> And you picked me up in a South Wales street,
> You only read *my* handwriting,
> And I write only to *you*.

I also started another factual poem:

> I kissed you by the Fragonard
> And all the lights went out.

But after that brisk opening my Muse went into retirement.

[8]

I greatly enjoyed my early work on Hugh Walpole, and few biographers can have had such abundant material to work on. Hugh kept a daily diary for most of his life, and sometimes a more expansive journal as well. I quickly realised that I couldn't read all that more than once, so I filled one large notebook with an exact chronology of where Hugh was on every day of his life, and in five other notebooks I made a précis of every date, fact and quotation which might be useful. All this took the best part of two years but it was enjoyable work, and only once or twice afterwards did I have to verify something in the diaries.

Then there were the letters, two trunkfuls of them entirely unsorted. Apart from enjoying reading them I learned the handwriting and identity of all the writers, except for half a dozen inscrutable scribbles. The most interesting letters were seventy-eight from Henry James, seventy-three from Arnold Bennett, sixty from Virginia Woolf, fifty from John Galsworthy, thirty-two from Joseph Conrad, among others. My little back room in Connaught Street was perfect for this work, because there were no evening interruptions. All the diaries and letters are now in the Humanities Research Center at Austin, Texas.

[9]

On 4 October 1946 my sister Deirdre, whose first husband Ronnie Balfour had been killed during the war, married David Wolfers, who had been a prisoner of war. The wedding was in the Chelsea Register Office. I went with our father and other relations. We sat on one side of the waiting-room, the bridegroom's family opposite. When we had been kept waiting for half an hour my father said, 'Since we seem to have plenty of time, we might as well make arrangements for my funeral.' This made us laugh, but the Wolfers party were clearly scandalised.

Soon after this David's brother, Johnny Wolfers, came to the office, asking whether he could work for us without pay while he lived on his army gratuity and decided what he wanted to do. His arrival was a godsend, for we badly needed a helper but couldn't afford to pay for one. Johnny quickly mastered everything – driving the van, doing accounts, packing parcels of books, at which he was adept. He invented a way of getting parcels up to the ground floor quickly: one man in the cellar throwing each parcel to a man halfway up the stairs, who threw it to another above. Johnny called this *la chaine humaine*. His quick wit, willingness to do anything, and wonderful sense of humour brightened our lives, and when he left after three years, by which time he was earning six pounds a week, we missed him sorely. Never can an infant firm have had such a rewarding helper.

[10]

The year 1947 opened with energy and excitement over the approaching publication of the firm's first two books. Then, early in March, we had an unexpected visit from Stephen Potter, whom David and I had known before the war, when Cape published his entertaining account of the teaching of English literature in universities, *The Muse in Chains*. Now he was working for the Third Programme of the BBC, which, owing to some dispute, had just been out of action for most of a month. Stephen used this unexpected leisure to rough out, on little scraps of paper, a short book which he thought would amuse us. He brought the scraps with him and read them aloud. We laughed so much that we immediately offered to publish the book, had it illustrated in exactly the right way by my friend Frankie Wilson, collected every ream of paper we could buy (luckily it was a short book), printed 25,000 copies, and, without realising that we were introducing a new word into the English language, on 4 November 1947 we published *The Theory and Practice of Gamesmanship, or The Art of Winning Games Without Actually Cheating* – our second financial winner.

[11]

It was difficult for Ruth and me to meet very often in London. She had her family to look after, I my publishing business, but there was the telephone and the prompt delivery of letters (I sent her ninety-two during 1947), and occasionally a thrilling lunch in what we quickly came to call 'our room'.

Then came a great opportunity. Ruth was staying with some old friends at Neath in Glamorgan, and she telephoned to her family to tell them she was staying an extra four days. We arranged to meet at Newport, Monmouthshire, on Friday 7 March. I was to drive up there the day before, but was prevented by one of the heaviest snowfalls of the century. Luckily the railways were still functioning, however slowly, and I took all day getting to Newport with many changes. During a stop at Gloucester I sent Ruth a telegram saying: TRAINING SLOWLY BUT SURELY. ALL PLANS HOLD GOOD.

I spent the night in the King's Head at Newport, and Ruth, by train from Neath, joined me there next morning. We lunched in the hotel and then forced our way to the railway station and a train to Abergavenny. The journey took a long time, during which I taught Ruth how to tackle crossword puzzles, which she had never before attempted to do. On the steep little hill from Abergavenny station to the town they had cut a path through the snow just wide enough for one person to walk down on it. Ruth went ahead and I followed, carrying our suitcases. The Angel was a delightful hotel. We had a fine comfortable bedroom, and the food was good. An attentive waiter kept trying to persuade us to buy black-market cigarettes.

This was the first time we had been able to spend a whole night together, and to have four running was blissful, as were the four whole days. We went for short walks in the snow, shopped at Woolworth's, and one evening visited the local cinema. Ruth said that those four days and nights were the greatest thing that had ever happened to her. The complete bill for four days and nights and all food came to £13 8*s* 3*d*.

[12]

I told Comfort of my love for Ruth, and she said that in one way she was relieved, since she had been worrying about my almost four years of celibacy. But she begged me not to break up the family and I promised not to. That promise was kept.[1] Ruth had similarly told her husband. He was naturally upset but was prepared to consider the whole thing a passing fancy and not to dwell on it.

We longed to elope and start a new life somewhere else, but we realised we couldn't possibly leave our children (my Adam was only four) and decided that we would just see as much of each other as possible, hoping that one day we should be together all the time.

David Garnett had started my publishing firm by suggesting it, and now he gave me a second great encouragement. In June we had our first glimpse of the Promised Land, the beautiful wide valley of Swaledale in the North Riding of Yorkshire. David lent us for a week his rented cottage called Butts Intake, high on the side of the dale. It was primitive but cosy, overlooking the village of Low Row, way down on the road below. The view up the dale was stupendous and we both fell in love with the dale. We bought eggs and milk from the nearest farm, and clambered down to Low Row, where the benevolent grocer sold us sugar and far more butter than our ration-books allowed. Thereafter we returned to Swaledale every summer for a brief holiday.

[13]

In 1948 we published sixteen books, starting with *Slocum* and ending with the complete novels of Thomas Love Peacock in one volume. This was edited by David, but I spent many days in the British Museum, ferreting out information for footnotes, which were all credited to David. This work was admirable training for the thousands of footnotes I manufactured in later years.

On 11 March I wrote to Ruth: 'It was perfect of you to look after D. Poor lamb, compared with her torpid indecision, I feel myself

1 Until the children were grown up I almost always went down to Bromsden Farm on Friday evening and left on Monday morning. Every summer I took them all to the seaside.

(with my unwritten book, unprofitable business, disappearing bedroom, disappearing exchequer and double life) to be a rock of balance and calm good sense.' The disappearing bedroom was the cosy one in Connaught Street, which Mary Booker now wanted for one of her daughters. Through Deirdre's kindness I spent all my weekday nights for the next two years in a basement bedroom in her house in Wellington Square, Chelsea.

When I went home for the Easter weekend, Adam was sitting in the car at Henley station, eating an ice. When he saw me he said: 'Dad, when we get home I'll give you four hundred kisses.' Luckily this rash promise was soon forgotten.

In May Ruth and I spent three weeks at Butts Intake. There, having finished my preparatory work on Hugh Walpole, I drafted the first three chapters of my book, Ruth typing each page as I finished it. Whenever I stuck at a difficult passage Ruth said: 'Just write down what you want to say in the fewest possible words, and then pass on. You can easily revise it later if necessary.' Funnily enough almost all those passages got through unchanged, and the draft chapters were scarcely altered at all.

In June I spent some days with my dear friend Wyndham Ketton-Cremer in his lovely old house Felbrigg Hall, near Cromer in Norfolk. A booksellers' conference was in progress at nearby Sheringham, and on the last day I went there and made another speech on behalf of the new small publisher, which was well received.

In August first Adam and then Bridget went down with chicken-pox, thus destroying our plans for a summer holiday by the sea.

One morning in September, walking from Paddington station to Connaught Street, I trod on a defective manhole-cover, which gave way, precipitating me on to the pavement with an injured ankle and a nasty gash in my leg. This caused me to spend several days in the Henley Memorial Hospital, having twenty painful injections of penicillin and a little operation with an anaesthetic. I had by this time got through a few more chapters of Hugh, and as soon as I was home again I began an account of his time in Russia during the First World War.

In November I spent a few days with Hugh's sister and brother, Dorothy and Robin Walpole, at their house in Corstorphine on the outskirts of Edinburgh. Dorothy was still working hard as a doctor. They were both naturally very interested in my book and approved of what I'd written. But when I read aloud a couple of chapters they both fell into a deep sleep.

One day I went over to the neighbouring village of Limberton, where in an untended cemetery I found the neglected grave of my dear friend Hamish Miles. I put two bunches of everlastings against the tombstone, one from me and one from Ruth, and then to the ambient air recited in a loud voice William Cory's lovely poem:

> They told me, Heraclitus, they told me you were dead,
> They brought me bitter news to hear and bitter tears to shed.
> I wept as I remember'd how often you and I
> Had tired the sun with talking and sent him down the sky.
> And now that thou art lying, my dear old Carian guest,
> A handful of grey ashes, long, long ago at rest,
> Still are thy pleasant voices, thy nightingales, awake;
> For Death, he taketh all away, but them he cannot take.

Then I said Goodbye and went back to the Walpoles.

[14]

The early months of 1949 brought us welcome new arrivals. First came David's son Richard Garnett, to help with production, editorial and other work: he was a pillar of the firm for most of its life. Then came Harry Townshend. He had been with Butterworth, the law publishers, for a year or two. For a long time his family had owned Simpkin Marshall, the largest and most important wholesalers in the book trade. It received a direct hit from a bomb in the war, and what was left was bought by the monster Robert Maxwell. He soon lost interest in it, and Harry was given leave from the army to close the firm down. He came to us as director in charge of sales and finance.

Then Book Tokens Ltd wrote to tell me that they were starting a new series of tokens for children, to be called Book Tallies, and asked whether my firm would undertake the choice and printing of designs on them. Yes, I said, sensing it was just the job for Ruth, who knew many artists, young and old, and had a splendid sense of design.

Richard and Harry shared a large table in Teddy's room, and Ruth had a little desk in mine. We were getting very crowded and began looking for larger offices.

Since we had no means of 'travelling' our books about the country, we persuaded a small firm called the Falcon Press to take our books along with theirs. Their London traveller Guy Fisher turned out to be the best in the country. Fairly soon he abandoned the Falcon Press and joined us full-time as our London representative. He was always cheerful and was very popular with all booksellers, who trusted him not to land them with piles of unsaleable books. He was, and is, the dearest of men, and he stayed with us for the rest of the firm's life.

In 1949 we published twenty-one books, including two by the brothers Maynard and Geoffrey Keynes, three more books by Henry James, and my uncle Duff Cooper's excellent little book *Sergeant Shakespeare*, in which he tried to prove that Shakespeare had been a serving soldier. This caused an outcry from Cape, who had an option on Duff's next book. Not knowing this I could only apologise, and they insisted on having an option on his following book. This was his only novel, *Operation Heartbreak*, which he was just finishing. He asked me how we could dodge Cape's option, and I told him that when he had finished the book he should send it to Cape, with a letter saying that he wanted an advance on royalties of £1,000, which they had paid for his *David*. Knowing Jonathan's meanness I felt sure he wouldn't pay so much, and sure enough he returned the manuscript to Duff with a note saying, 'I am wondering whether fiction is a really suitable medium for you . . . and that biography is really your field'. We published the book with resounding success in 1950.

Bridget on Grey Owl, her first horse

[15]

On the home front Bridget was given the first of her many horses – a mare called Grey Owl. Duff was in sight of his first half at Eton, and in April I went down with mumps, caught from Adam. He was up and about after a few days, but I was in bed for a month. At the end of May I recuperated by taking Ruth to Butts Intake for a fortnight, during which we drove round the Lake District, stopping at Brackenburn and Hugh Walpole's grave.

At the beginning of August I spent three days with Dorothy and Robin Walpole at Brackenburn and on 10 August we all attended the opening of the Hugh Walpole Collection in the Fitz Park Museum at Keswick, during which I made a short speech. The collection contained the manuscripts of all the Herries novels, Epstein's head of

Hugh, letters to him from thirteen leading English writers and a quantity of other memorabilia.

In September Ruth and I spent a weekend at Truro, visiting the places where Hugh had stayed as a child, and driving over to Polperro, where for some years he had a cottage overlooking the little harbour. All through the year I worked steadily at his biography, averaging a thousand words a day, and by 31 December I had finished the first draft of the book.

[16]

On 3 January 1950 I embarked on the *Queen Mary* to spend the rest of the month in New York, in search of books to publish. Leaving Ruth was agony for us both. Deirdre very sweetly came to see me off, so as to comfort Ruth in the first hours of her abandonment.

I travelled cabin-class, sharing a cabin with two agreeable men. The food was first-class, and cigarettes cost a shilling for twenty. Occasionally I climbed up to the first-class deck and had drinks with rich friends. The weather worsened daily, and the ship's officers said it was the roughest voyage the great ship had so far met. We were twenty-four hours late in reaching New York. An excellent remedy called Kwells effectively saved me from sea-sickness.

In New York I stayed with my friend Gerstle Mack in his apartment on East 55th Street. He had published lives of Cézanne and Courbet. He had only one bedroom and I slept on a comfortable divan in the living-room. Gerstle cooked excellent meals for me and looked after me tenderly in every way. On the evenings when he had a party of friends to play canasta I arranged to dine out.

I visited up to six publishers and literary agents each day. They all treated me to lavish lunches and dinners, and I was taken to all the plays I wanted to see – the first production of T.S. Eliot's *The Cocktail Party*, *Kiss Me Kate*, the dramatised version of Kate O'Brien's fine novel *That Lady* in which Katherine Cornell excelled, and most importantly *South Pacific*.

I reported to Ruth: 'Lunch at Alfred Knopf's country house was terrific – vodka, wild duck, Burgundy, cheese, Chateau Yquem, an incredibly good soufflé and a Churchillian cigar.' Ruth and I sent each other an airmail letter every day. They usually arrived in two days, sometimes three. I told her of my delight in *South Pacific*, and in particular the song 'Some Enchanted Evening', from which I quoted the line 'Once you have found her, never let her go'. Ruth was busy in the office, dealing with authors, answering letters to me, organising the firm and looking for larger premises all over central London.

Then came my first meeting with Leon Edel. He took me to an excellent French restaurant, where we talked for hours about Henry James and other authors and became firm friends for life. Later he gave me lunch in his tiny apartment near the hideous United Nations building, whose activities he was reporting daily in an evening paper called *PM*.

I saw a lot of my old friend Alistair Cooke and his wife Jane, arranging to publish two books of his. I visited Ralph Bates and travelled down to Stone Harbor, New Jersey, to spend an enjoyable night with the American novelist Joseph Hergesheimer and his wife in their seaside house, where the Atlantic breakers perpetually crashed down on seven miles of smooth flat sand.

Towards the end of my stay I wrote to Ruth from New York: 'Each time I visit this fantastic city I go through the same sequence of feelings – excitement, stimulus, gaiety, heavy cold, wretchedness, longing to be home.'

[17]

On the first morning of my return journey a young man came to my cabin, saying that his literary agent had told him to look me up. His name was Hugh Wheeler and he was an Englishman who lived in America. With his friend Richard Webb he had written many excellent detective stories under the names Patrick Quentin, Q. Patrick and Jonathan Stagge. Webb had retired because of illness, and Hugh was writing even better books on his own. Later he wrote plays and libretti for Stephen Sondheim (*A Little Night Music*) and others. I published his only non-detective novel, *The Crippled Muse,* and his first play.

Now on the rough Atlantic – not quite as rough as on the outward voyage, but needing ropes along all the passages and companion-ways for passengers to hold on to – Hugh and I spent most of our time in a deserted lounge, discussing books and trying, between us, to reconstruct famous poems aloud. His intelligent companionship made the voyage very agreeable, even when we were held up for hours at Cherbourg before my rapturous reunion with my beloved Ruth.

[18]

During 1950 we published twenty-five books, including *Elephant Bill* by J.H. Williams, two books by Eric Linklater, *Lifemanship* by Stephen Potter, *A Generation on Trial* (the case of Alger Hiss) by Alistair Cooke, the Collected Poems of Robert Louis Stevenson, *Operation Heartbreak,* and the first two volumes of The Reynard Library – a series of compendious volumes of great English writers beginning with Dr Johnson and Goldsmith, to be followed in successive years by Sterne, Browning, Dryden, Macaulay, Matthew Arnold, Wordsworth, Cardinal Newman, Carlyle, Fitzgerald and Cowper.

In April we found and leased the perfect house for our new offices, no. 36 Soho Square. The large basement we used for invoicing, packing and storing books. On the ground floor there was a large reception room which housed the telephone operator and three typists, with two smaller offices behind. On the first floor I had a huge office at the back (very useful for board meetings and such), off which was a tiny office for Ruth, and three good offices at the front of the house. On the second floor was a flat occupied by the actress Pamela Brown and three cats. On the top floor was a fine flat for me, with two bedrooms, a large sitting-room, kitchen and bathroom.

This was the haven that Ruth and I had so long been seeking, and after a blissful fortnight at Butts Intake we set about making the flat habitable. On the walls of the sitting-room there were at least six

36 Soho Square

thicknesses of wallpaper. About four down there was a gay William
Morris pattern, but we couldn't separate it, so all had to go. We found
an excellent man-of-all-trades called Mr Mills, a carpenter, painter,
plumber and general handyman.

And then the power of chance showed its hand. Teddy Young was
travelling from Redhill to London with Eileen (Paddy) McGrady who
had been a colleague at World Books. She told him that June Clifford,
who had helped us out on that Saturday morning four years ago, had

*Osbert Lancaster's
idea of the rush of
authors*

just spent two years in South Africa, where she had worked for a publishing firm and married an English optician called David Williams. Now he had come home to a job in London, and June was looking for work. Teddy told Paddy that I was desperately seeking a good secretary, after a number of duds, and told her that June should come and see me.

This she did, looking very small, neat, pretty and nervous. She was expecting me to cross-question her about her shorthand and typing ability, but the only question I asked her was: 'Are you in any immediate danger of having a baby?' She said she wasn't, and I told her that I had lost several secretaries through marriage or mother-hood. We chatted happily for a while, and then I asked her to start work the next Monday, which she did, and proved to be easily the best secretary I ever had in all my working life.

The flat was habitable by the end of the year, and I spent most of my evenings dividing *Hugh Walpole* into seven parts and twenty-six chapters.

*With Ruth and
Leon Edel outside
36 Soho Square*

[19]

In 1951 we published forty books, including *The Silver Locusts* by Ray Bradbury, the leading science-fiction writer in America, Alistair Cooke's *Letters from America*, and my old friend Allan Wade's bibliography of the works of W.B. Yeats, which became the first volume of The Soho Bibliographies, a surprisingly successful series. In July Ruth and I spent three happy weeks at Butts Intake. After we got back Ruth wrote to me: 'The realisation of the utter blissful peace of our weeks together comes over me more and more. We slip into it with such relaxed entirety that when it is over I don't believe it, but feel a numbed emptiness which seems to permit of no real wish to do anything except just be left alone. And that is impossible. I should so much like to thank you for the most heavenly three weeks of my life.'

And soon afterwards I wrote to her: 'I wasn't meant to be a publisher, darling, but rather some dimmish man of letters, reading and researching a lot, writing a little. Starting the firm was fun, but holding it up for ever, like Atlas, is a dismal expectation.' I had to endure this for another thirteen years before my dreams came true.

At Bromsden Farm Grey Owl, much to Bridget's joy and excitement, produced a foal, a fine bay colt. But soon we had to drag her away from horse-fancying, when at the beginning of September Comfort and I took the three children for a fortnight's holiday at l'Auberge du Vieux Puits at Puys, two miles along the coast from Dieppe. The superb food was cooked by the *patron* himself, and one day he invited us into his kitchen, where we were surrounded by vats of cream, herbs and other delicacies. He turned a great bowl of cream upside down and said proudly: '*Voilà – ça ne bouge pas!*'

The children bathed and played on the sandy beach, and we found a tennis-club where most of us could play. On Saturday mornings we explored the busy market in Dieppe, and the holiday was enjoyed by all.

[20]

Early in January 1952 I set out on another book-hunting journey to America. This time I went by air, my first long flight. It was before the time of jets, and I travelled in BOAC Stratocruiser Speedbird, which had two huge propellers half-way down each side of the body. My fear of flying, which has never left me, was slightly allayed by a lunch of aperitif, turtle soup, salmon mayonnaise, hot casserole of chicken, coffee and brandy, but my spirits dropped again at the news that we were being diverted to Iceland.

As we descended towards the dismal-looking island I saw before us a flat surface of ice, stretching out of sight. Realising that if brakes were applied when we hit the ground we should shoot on into the sea, I nervously asked the co-pilot how they stopped the machine, and he told me that they pressed two buttons which put the two inboard propellers into reverse, thus reducing the speed to nil, and sure enough we landed at Keflavik with smooth certainty, without a skid. The Americans had built a gigantic airfield there, adjacent to which was a large overheated air-terminal, containing, among other things, a post office and a coffee-bar, against which a host of American GIs were leaning in extreme boredom, partly because all Iceland was teetotal. The windows were almost completely blocked by snow.

A BOAC Stratocruiser

I had some coffee and bought some postcards, which I despatched to family and friends saying 'Here I am in Iceland'. After a wait of a good two hours we re-embarked on the Stratocruiser, only to be told, soon after we had taken off, that we were now to be diverted to Gander, in Newfoundland, Canada. The terminal at Gander was much like the one in Iceland, but it contained a bar which was open all day and night. I drank three Canadian Club whiskies and smoked my pipe. I was quickly learning that air-travel turns the romance of all countries into a series of hideous hot waiting-rooms.

After a long wait there we eventually reached the USA. A wait of an hour in customs and then we finally reached New York. The journey from London had taken twenty-four hours.

It was 6.30 a.m. before I reached the house where I was to stay with Betty Hines, rich widow and a cousin of Comfort's. I was horrified to learn that her chauffeur had been waiting up for me all night. I took a sleeping draught and slept deeply for four and a half hours, after which an English butler, the sure sign of wealthy Americans, brought me a delicious breakfast in bed. After a bath I dressed, saw Betty for a few minutes, then explored the house, which had a Renoir on every landing, two Gauguins and a Daumier. Betty told me to order lunch for myself, but I didn't feel hungry.

The British Book Centre gave me a tiny room with a telephone in it, on which I spoke to Alistair Cooke, Leon Edel and other friends. Comfort's sister Emmy Hall telephoned from Boston, where her husband Ham was recovering from a serious operation, so I changed my plans, took a train to Boston, spent a day with Emmy, visited the convalescent husband, stayed at the Statler Hotel, and then visited all the publishers and literary agents in Boston, after which my friend Bill Jackson, the librarian of the Houghton Library, drove me over the river to Harvard, where I visited the publishers at the University Press.

Then back to New York, where I visited five publishers on the same day, and spent a happy evening with Ralph Bates and his wife.

Betty Hines was all kindness and generosity, but I didn't much enjoy the number of dinner-parties in rich people's houses to which she took me. I wrote to Ruth: 'Rich Americans are really frightful. How paradoxical that in order to find a house full of servants and real social snobbery one should have to come to this land where "democracy" is a fetish.'

But there was one bright light at Betty's, for she was a sister-in-law of Adlai Stevenson, the best President the Americans never elected, and he was a frequent visitor to the house. I took a great liking to him and later published four of his books.

One evening, after visiting many publishers, I went with Betty's daughter Joanie to see Gertrude Lawrence and Yul Brynner in *The King and I*, during which I twice fell asleep. I spent happy evenings with Alistair and Jane Cooke, Leslie Hotson and others.

One day Leon Edel drove me out to his new home at Jamaica, some fourteen miles from New York. We had been discussing the bibliography of Henry James, on which he was already engaged. As we drove over the Triborough Bridge he told me that an assistant or co-editor would be a great help, and at Rutgers University he had come across a very intelligent and literary-minded young man called Dan Laurence. In due course he worked with Leon on the bibliography and became a lifelong friend of mine, before he became the world expert on the life, letters and work of George Bernard Shaw.

Then came a sad letter from June, saying that her husband had been appointed manager of a branch of his firm in Cheltenham, and she would have to cease being my secretary before the end of February – a terrible blow.

On went the whirlpool of publishers and parties: at one given by Blanche Knopf, the wife of Alfred the publisher, I met Oscar Hammerstein II, who collaborated with Richard Rodgers in so many good musicals. I asked him which was written first, the words or the music. He said usually the words, but occasionally Rodgers wrote the words as well as the music. Hammerstein told me that he had written all the words of *South Pacific* before they were set to music. I told him I thought 'Some Enchanted Evening' was the most beautiful of them all.

I went to *Guys and Dolls*, which I greatly enjoyed, and spent one whole afternoon in the secondhand bookshops in Lower Fourth

Avenue, buying many books cheaply. Ruth and I wrote to each other every day of the month, and her letters were a great encouragement to me. Once again I had bought the English rights of only a few books, though my visit seemed to have been a success, but it was with delight that I embarked on another frightening flight home on 6 February. Ruth had arranged to meet me in London, but fog caused us to be diverted to Shannon Airport in Ireland, where the owners of the airline stood us all unlimited drinks.

[21]

The most exciting event of the next weeks was the publication of *Hugh Walpole* on 4 March. It produced a torrent of letters and reviews, most of them laudatory. In those days many reviews were anonymous, but several well-known authors swelled the chorus – Peter Quennell, Edwin Muir, Tony Powell (a whole page in *The Times Literary Supplement*), Cyril Connolly, Rose Macaulay, Frank Swinnerton, Harold Nicolson, but much the most perceptive was Michael Sadleir's in the *Spectator*. He was almost the only reviewer who realised what a difficult book this had been to write.

When the American edition was published by the Macmillan Company in August, the reviews were as numerous and encouraging as the English ones. Dear old Sam Behrman wrote: 'I would willingly give my eye-teeth (whatever those may be) to have written this book.' Altogether there have been six different editions of it, three in America and three over here, where Hamish Hamilton published it as a paperback. Macmillan, bless them, kept the original edition in print for eighteen years.

I was soon back at work in Soho Square, but without dear June at my side. In July Ruth and I spent another heavenly holiday at Butts Intake. One day we drove fifty-five miles to Saltburn, a delightful little Victorian town on the east coast, twenty miles north of Whitby. We bathed in an icy sea and spent the rest of the day in deck-chairs on the beach.

In September Ruth left for a fortnight's holiday in Provence with her husband and children. We wrote to each other every day, but while she was away I had a host of troubles. Alan Bott died on 17 September, aged fifty-eight, and I became Hugh Walpole's sole literary executor, which I remained until his copyright expired in 1991.[1] I did my best to comfort Alan's darling wife Jo, attended the funeral and made all the arrangements for the memorial service at St Martin-in-the-Fields, which was very well attended.

At the same time, when copies of G.M. Young's life of Stanley Baldwin had been printed, both Winston and Beaverbrook threatened to sue for libel if certain passages were not removed or altered. I sought help from Arnold Goodman, a brilliant lawyer, who had been a partner in my and Cape's solicitor's firm Rubinstein Nash. He was immensely helpful and kept me fairly calm (in later years he was to become one of my greatest benefactors). I also visited Sir Norman Brook in the Cabinet Office. Eventually some sort of compromise was agreed, and John Sparrow and I fudged up the right number of words to replace the offending sentences. This entailed the removal of seven leaves from each of the 7,580 copies of the book, and the insertion of the reprinted pages instead – a hideously expensive operation.

We published thirty-seven books in 1952, which included Teddy Young's *One of Our Submarines*, Guy Chapman's life of Beckford, poems by Andrew Young, books by Leslie Hotson and Ray Bradbury, and Stephen Potter's *One-Upmanship*, of which we sold 20,000 copies before publication.

[22]

The year 1953 was one of varied fortunes. The firm's finances were rocky, through insufficiency of capital, and we were obliged to rearrange everything, which meant that our original investors would lose a good deal of their money.

---

1 It has now been extended to 2011.

This unhappily made David, the originator of the whole business, turn against me. He accused me of dishonesty and fraud, and sent an aggressive business friend of his to cross-examine me. His chief accusation was that I was living in the flat at the firm's expense. I told him that the rent of the flat was £150 a year, and that the Walpole family, in recognition of all my work on Hugh's estate and copyrights, were paying £200 a year *to the firm*, to cover my rent, rates, electricity and telephone. The emissary retired discomfited, but my long friendship with David was broken.

This meant goodbye to Butts Intake, so Ruth and I rented a cottage in the village of Thwaite, further up the dale, at the foot of the hill called Kisdon, and spent a happy fortnight there.

In August I took Comfort and the children to a house called Craig Rock, on the coast, near Bognor Regis. They all loved it. One day we visited Arthur Ransome and his wife on their yacht in Itchenor harbour.

Then in September we published a translation from the German called *Seven Years in Tibet* by Heinrich Harrer. In all it sold over 200,000 copies, by far the largest sale in the firm's history. Also in that year we published Duff Cooper's *Old Men Forget* and the first volume of Leon Edel's life of Henry James.

[23]

In the middle of May 1954 Ruth and I again rented the cottage at Thwaite, from which we searched the landscape for a cottage of our own. The only difference between cottages and barns was that the cottages had chimneys. One day, struggling up the steep slope of Kisdon, we spotted a cottage almost at the top of the great hill. It was derelict, but if it could be bought and resurrected it was just the place for us, with wonderful views in three directions. It took us months to discover who owned it and the two large adjoining fields. It was an old lady living hundreds of miles away and she was prepared to sell. We then persuaded a charming local farmer Willie Whitehead to buy, on the understanding that we would buy the cottage from him,

Ruth at Kisdon

leaving him with the two fields. A little later I came across these lines
from W.H. Auden's poem 'Streams':

> Lately, in that dale of all Yorkshire's the loveliest,
> Where, off its fell-side helter-skelter, Kisdon Beck
> Jumps into Swale with a boyish shouting,
> Sprawled out on grass, I dozed for a second.

In June Ruth and her husband went to Menton on the south coast of France. He immediately fell seriously ill and Ruth had to nurse him, day and night, for six weeks. She was kept going by daily swims in the sea, by the letters which we wrote to each other every day, and by our twice-weekly telephone calls.

While she was away I spent a weekend at Chantilly, my first visit there since Duff's death in January. Diana, as ever, was the perfect hostess, and the other guests were Rosamond Lehmann, David and Rachel Cecil, and Enid Bagnold. One day for lunch came General Lord 'Pug' Ismay, who regaled us with anecdotes about Winston. My favourite was of their travelling together in a car, in which Winston rehearsed the speech he was to give in the House of Commons on 20 August 1940 after the Battle of Britain. When he came to the famous sentence, 'Never in the history of mankind have so many owed so much to so few', Ismay said: 'What about Jesus Christ and his disciples?' 'Good old Pug,' said Winston, who immediately changed the wording to 'Never in the field of human conflict . . .'.

At the end of June I gave a dinner for Henry James's nephew Billy and his wife at the Garrick Club. H.J.'s old secretary Theodora Bosanquet was one of eight in the party. As I wrote to Ruth: 'We had smoked salmon, very good lamb with lots of veg, strawberries and cream, with sherry, claret and brandy.' The bill for the eight of us came to £13 14s 3d. Those were the days.

On 20 July Ruth at last succeeded in bringing the invalid home to Hampstead, where their daughter Jill had engaged day and night nurses. We felt a desperate need to be alone together, so we slipped away to a comfortable hotel at Worthing on the Sussex coast, where we spent two blissful days and nights.

At the end of August I took Comfort and the children for a fortnight to the Hôtel Beau Rivage at Loctudy on the south coast of Brittany. We drove 300 miles each way. After crossing by night from Southampton to St Malo, we breakfasted at Honfleur, where the children were delighted by a ten-egg omelette. At Loctudy the children greatly enjoyed a sardine-canning factory, but they spent most of their time on the beach or eating the hotel's superb food. One day we drove to Quimper and went over the pottery factory.

In 1954 we published forty-one books, including *Son of Oscar Wilde* by Wilde's son Vyvyan Holland, *The Letters of W.B. Yeats*, edited by my dear old friend Allan Wade, Ray Bradbury's *Fahrenheit 451*, *Three Singles to Adventure* and *The Bafut Beagles* by Gerald Durrell, who became one of our most regular and successful authors. Altogether we published eight books by Gerry; all popular but *My Family and Other Animals* (1956) was easily the most successful. Our original printing of 30,000 was sold almost immediately.

Gerry was looking for a place to set up a Wildlife Conservation Trust, and I introduced him to my army friend Hugh Fraser, who had an estate in Jersey which he wanted to sell. They agreed terms and the Jersey Wildlife Preservation Trust was established and is still thriving. Gerry made me an honorary member of it.

I suggested to Vyvyan that Allan Wade would be just the man to edit the Letters of Oscar Wilde. He agreed and Allan set out on his long task.

[24]

The eventful year of 1955 began with the deaths of two dear old friends. In February Humphry House, a brilliant scholar, lecturer in English at Oxford and Fellow of Wadham College, who knew more of the nineteenth century than anyone, died suddenly at the age of forty-six. In 1949 I had persuaded him to edit a complete edition of Dickens's letters and we had obtained a grant of £6,000 from the Pilgrim Trust. He had already transcribed 10,000 letters, but there was a great deal more work to be done.[1]

In April my beloved old comrade Charlie Marford died of cancer in his home outside Newton Abbot. I made two brief trips there to comfort his widow Molly.

---

1 The edition is still in progress, and Volume 9 appeared in 1997.

At the beginning of May Ruth and I drove off to our most exciting three weeks in Swaledale, for Willie Whitehead had succeeded in buying the cottage and fields. We visited him and he agreed to sell us the cottage for £250, to be paid in five annual instalments of £50. Off we drove to Willie's lawyer in Richmond, who gave us the title-deeds, but the cottage had no name. On the other side of Kisdon, above Muker, there were already Kisdon Farm and Kisdon Cottage, so we named our cottage Kisdon Lodge.

As the previous year we were staying in the Thwaite cottage and made great friends with Miss Lane and Mr Moody, who ran the village shop. They told us they had a large empty outhouse, in which we could store furniture as we bought it. Then we sought out Percy Calvert, the builder at Gunnerside, down the dale. He said he would come and inspect the cottage for us, and next day he turned up with his assistant Ken Barningham. They both spent an hour examining the building and were astonished at the dryness of interior and the solidity of walls and roof. 'Can you make this fit to live in?' I asked Percy. 'Aye,' said he, 'I'll fettle it up for ye.' Then glancing at the downstairs floor, which had harboured sheep for thirty winters, he pointed to the foot-deep mass of straw and sheep-droppings and said: 'We'll have to get a woman to clear this up', and sure enough two elderly ladies trudged up, removed everything and scrubbed the flagstones beneath.

Percy said he would do all the work in two months, and he told us that in the village of Keld, below us at the head of the dale, we would find a farmer called Bobbie Hutchinson, who would do everything and anything for us. This proved to be true, and Bobbie, his wife Ivy, and their son Billy became the dearest of friends. Bobbie was the kindest, nicest and most generous man I have ever known.

Percy said the whole operation would cost £150–£170. We told him that was too much and asked him to write out an itemised estimate. This he did, dropping the total to £115, but, by removing two 'luxuries', we got it down to £102.

Bobbie and Ivy Hutchinson

Next we attended every village sale to buy contents for the cottage – a large double bed for £5 10*s*, a strong kitchen table for 10*s*, three chairs (13*s*), an Aladdin lamp (one pound) and so on.

We shopped in Richmond, where we found a first-rate cobbler, who mended my old army boots in five minutes and charged sixpence. He *threw* handfuls of nails into his mouth, whisking them out singly and banging them in with one motion. He said different sorts of nails had different tastes, but they all used to taste much better.

At the end of June 1955 Ruth took her husband for a fortnight to Winchelsea in Sussex. This was the only time in the year when we needed to write to each other, which we did every day.

In July my dear old friend Allan Wade died suddenly after a happy day in the sunshine. He had made good progress with the Oscar Wilde letters, but there was clearly a great deal more to be done. With the approval of Vyvyan Holland I recklessly said that I would finish the job. It occupied most of my spare time during the next seven years.

[25]

On the last day of August we drove excitedly northwards (the car packed tight with furniture and other domestic objects) and spent a very comfortable night in a guest-house in Wensley, run by Mr and Mrs Gilbert Bullard, whose house it was. We had a delightful bedroom overlooking the garden, a bathroom with plenty of hot water, a good supper, an excellent breakfast, and the general comfort and atmosphere of a private house in the country. Our bill for the whole thing came to £2 8s.

After breakfast we drove to Gunnerside, got the key of Kisdon Lodge from Percy Calvert, and drove to the foot of Kisdon, where we left the laden car. It was lovely to see the cottage no longer blind but equipped with neat windows. The walls inside were just as we had chosen – pale blue downstairs and pale pink up. The workmen had made a splendid job of the doors and fireplaces. We ate our sandwich

Ruth at Kisdon Lodge

lunch happily in the porch, then walked down and met Billy Hutchinson with a jeep and tractor. We stowed all the contents of the car into them for Billy to drive up, then drove to Thwaite to rescue all the furniture and other things which our friends had housed for us. An amiable visitor from Sunderland managed to strap the kitchen table on to the roof of the car. When all was unpacked and more or less in place we were almost too excited to arrange all the minor objects. Excitement and a gale outside gave us a fitful night, the first in our very own home.

The next two days we were busy inside and out, and on each night we slept for eleven hours. Then, tidying everything up, we had to leave the place that was to be our joy and our earthly paradise for the next nine years.

[26]

On 18 October 1955, at a dinner-party given by Tim and Rosalie Nugent at their home in Chelsea Square, I met George Lyttelton, the only Eton master who had ever inspired me. He told me that in his Suffolk retirement nobody ever wrote to him. 'I'll write to you, George', I said, and after that I wrote to him almost every weekend and he answered every mid-week. Altogether we exchanged some six hundred letters until his death in 1962. I told George that my letters were the diary I never kept, and so they were, for my multifarious activities produced enough to fill a decent letter every week. I do not propose to describe all that again, and anyone who wants to read it must seek those published volumes. Here I shall only mention the highlights and important events.

[27]

By this time the firm's finances were rocky, and our only hope of survival seemed to be amalgamation with a larger firm. We tried several without success until we met a remarkable man called Lionel Fraser. Starting from nowhere he had become managing director of merchant banks, several city companies and, most important of all, Thomas Tilling, a very successful bus company. In 1948 Lionel sold all the buses and set up Thomas Tilling Ltd as an investment conglomerate. In 1955 they owned 40 per cent of William Heinemann Ltd[1] in which I had long ago spent two years as an office boy. Since the death of Charley Evans in 1944 the firm had steadily declined because the people running it lacked both literary flair and business acumen.

Lionel somehow took a fancy to me and decided I was just the right person to be chairman of Heinemann's. Thrice did he offer me that kingly crown, and thrice did I refuse, for I knew that books were all I was interested in, and the higher one got in any business the more one was absorbed in finance and administration.

So, before the end of 1955 Heinemann bought all the shares of our company and we became a subsidiary of theirs, keeping our editorial authority, our offices in Soho Square, and our invaluable London representative Guy Fisher.

In that year, 1955, we had published forty-six books, including *The Dreyfus Case* by Guy Chapman, *The Film of Memory* by Maurice Druon, *Switch on the Night* by Ray Bradbury, and Gavin Maxwell's first book *Harpoon at a Venture*.

Early in the year, in order to help reduce the firm's overheads, Teddy Young had volunteered to resign his directorship and find alternative employment. For a time he worked for the printing firm of Hazell, Watson and Viney at Aylesbury, with a brief to improve their 'in-house' typographical standards. A year later he joined the newly established publishing firm of Rainbird McLean, and many years later became its managing director. Meanwhile in Soho Square young Richard Garnett took over the production and design job he had been understudying under Teddy's tuition.

---

1 By the end of the 1950s they owned the whole firm.

[28]

In 1956 and the two following years we published a hundred and twenty-four books, all of which I had to read, and often edit, punctuate and even rewrite. I was still struggling with the Oscar Wilde letters and was on several committees.

The Heinemann merger had been announced in the press early in the year. As the year advanced it became apparent that we had made a big mistake. One of the advantages we had been promised was a substantial reduction in the cost of our overheads. In Soho Square we had employed two non-union packers, and all orders from bookshops anywhere were despatched, or in London delivered by van, within twenty-four hours. After the Heinemann take-over the twenty-four hours became three weeks, which lost us many sales in London, and the cost of packing shot up, since their packers were all union men, paid London union rates, though the packing was done at Kingswood, deep in Surrey.

On 18 March Ruth's husband Oliver Simon died after a long illness. This set Ruth free, her children were grown up, and she and I were more together than had been possible before.

PART TWO: LOVE AND TAXES

Oh, thou art fairer than the evening air
Clad in the beauty of a thousand stars;
Brighter art thou than flaming Jupiter
When he appeared to hapless Semele:
More lovely than the monarch of the sky
In wanton Arethusa's azured arms:
And none but thou shall be my paramour.

MARLOWE

[1]

LOVE WAS RUTH, and taxes were the problem of the London Library. In July I was out of the blue involved in the plight of the Library, which in the eighty years of its existence had been registered a tax-free charity. Now it suddenly received a demand from the Westminster City Council for annual rates of £2,481; in a few months this was increased to £4,963, which in its present position the Library couldn't afford. We immediately launched an appeal and engaged an excellent and very nice counsel, Geoffrey Lawrence QC, to act on our behalf.

In the interval I suggested that we should ask all the leading publishers to give the Library the books of theirs it needed instead of charging for them. I visited forty of the leading publishers and all but two of them agreed with the proposal, which saved the Library £3,500 a year.

My most amusing visit was to the most tight-fisted of all publishers, Sir Stanley Unwin. After I had explained the plan to him he immediately said that his principles would not allow him to agree. 'Once a publisher starts giving away books, he's lost.' After some discussion I left him, saying 'Thank you for seeing me, Sir Stanley, and when you've thought the matter over I'm sure your good nature will defeat your principles.' And by heaven it did!

At the beginning of August we dashed up again for another heavenly weekend on Kisdon. At the end of the month Comfort and I took Bridget and Adam to France for three weeks. Duff was doing his Military Service with the Coldstream Guards in Germany. We drove 500 miles to Hendaye, a delightful little French town on the northern border of Spain. A first-rate hotel with excellent food, a good bookshop and a fine sandy beach. Perfect weather all the time. We drove several times into Spain, beautiful country with an armed policeman at every crossroads. The holiday was thoroughly enjoyed by all ranks.

In 1956 we published forty-five books, including *My Family and Other Animals, The Letters of William Blake*, edited by Geoffrey Keynes, two fine historical novels by Maurice Druon and *The October Country* by Ray Bradbury.

[2]

In 1957, a very busy year, I was just at the end of editing and annotating the letters of George Moore to Lady Cunard, and selecting Edmund Blunden's poems for a collected volume, but I was still knee-deep in the Letters of Oscar Wilde, on which dear Allan Wade had made a splendid start. Tracking down original letters involved correspondence with universities, libraries, booksellers, book-owners and auctioneers all over the world. Luckily I could dictate all these enquiries to my secretary in office hours.

Our London Library appeal was heard at the Westminster Valuation Court on 26 July and was turned down on 22 August. We immediately lodged an appeal with the Lands Tribunal.

At the end of August I spent half my fiftieth birthday at Rapallo with Max Beerbohm's widow Elisabeth and half with Ruth and her daughter at Cagnes-sur-Mer.

In September I received a charming letter from Harold Nicolson, asking if I would succeed him as Chairman of the Committee of the London Library. The dear man was getting very deaf and was appalled by the onset of the Inland Revenue demand. I accepted with alacrity, and despite all my other activities I proudly held the post for twelve long years.

During the year we published fifty-five books (the most in any year so far). They included *Union Street* by Charles Causley, *Invasion 1940* (his first historical work) by Peter Fleming and *A Sociable Plover* by Eric Linklater.

[3]

The following year was one of turmoil – committees, lectures, the London Library, the Literary Society (a dining club founded by Wordsworth and others, of which I was secretary and treasurer, ordering all the meals, etc., at the Garrick Club).

On New Year's Day I talked for three-quarters of an hour to the Hove Quill Club on Oscar Wilde. I had prepared nothing, but simply let loose on them a hurricane of words, facts and quotations, which seemed to go down reasonably well.

With Duff at Oxford and Adam at Eton my overdraft soared. In February I spent a week-end at Chantilly, going through with Diana Cooper the proofs of *The Rainbow Comes and Goes*, the first volume of her memoirs. I then wrote a profile of her which appeared in the *Sunday Times*. Leon Edel, Alistair Cooke and Elisabeth Beerbohm came over for visits and occupied, very enjoyably, a good deal of my time.

After attending the Fourth of June at Eton, with Eric and Marjorie Linklater, Ruth and I drove off for three blessed weeks at Kisdon, where we steadily slept for twelve hours on most nights. Ruth filled the cottage with wild flowers. We had with us two large cartons of Oscar Wilde material, and on every evening and wet day I sweated away at the final notes and so on. We shopped at Hawes in Wensleydale and visited the second-hand bookshop there, where I bought the first four volumes of the *Cornhill Magazine*, beautifully bound, for six shillings.

Then came the most exciting of our village sales. It was at Bagby near Thirsk, and we bought a lovely eighteenth-century grandfather clock, which had been made at Thirsk. We paid £1 for it[1] and 3*s* for a coloured picture of a ship worked in wool. We lashed the clock on to the roof of the car and Bobbie brought it up to the cottage in his tractor. It took us several days to fix the clock at its proper level, and then its delicious tick gave us very peaceful pleasure. Those blissfully happy days gave me fresh energy for all the London Library and other tasks ahead.

On 30 June T.S. Eliot, as President of the London Library, and I as Chairman of the Committee, gave evidence before the Lands Tribunal. Then he and I presided over the Annual General Meeting of the Library. After two hours of question and answer all present agreed to increase the annual subscription of members from six guineas to ten. The following month the Lands Tribunal turned down our appeal, and after a discussion with Geoffrey Lawrence we decided to try our luck with the Court of Appeal. I managed to persuade the Library Committee to approve this.

Among all these alarms and excursions Ruth and I managed two brief visits to our beloved Kisdon with a mass of Oscar Wilde material, on which I did a lot of work whenever it rained.

At the end of September, after I had made a speech to the Library Association at Brighton, Ruth and I attended Tom Eliot's seventieth birthday party in the Eliots' flat: only twelve there. I persuaded Epstein to propose Tom's health, which he did very well. Then I told Tom he must blow out all the candles on the birthday cake at one puff, which he obediently did. Then he said very simply: 'This is the happiest birthday I've ever had.'

Quite soon, after attending a friend's funeral in Wiltshire, I boldly invited myself to lunch with Siegfried Sassoon, who lived nearby. We got on splendidly and became firm friends for the rest of his life.

---

1 Thirty years later Sotheby's valued it at £400–600.

The year ended with another sad death, that of Hugh Walpole's sister Dorothy. She had worked satisfactorily all her life as a doctor. In her will, bless her, she left me £1,000, which enormously helped with my son's school fees.

[4]

The next year, 1959, opened with the sad news of the death of Elisabeth Beerbohm, a darling woman. It soon transpired that she had left no will, so everything she owned, including Max's royalties and copyrights, now belonged to her equally darling sister Eva Reichmann.

In the middle of March I was the guest of honour at the annual dinner of the Manchester Society of Book-Collectors, to whom I made a speech.

At last the law's delays came to an end when on 12 October three judges of the Court of Appeal turned down the Library's appeal with a 'judgment reserved' which was delivered a fortnight later. Clearly they were all on the Library's side, but the law was not. During that time Eliot was in America, so other friends and I concocted a letter for publication in *The Times*. T.S.E. got back in time to approve it, and it duly appeared over his and my signatures on 5 November, to be backed up by letters from Winston Churchill, John Masefield, the Poet Laureate, and other notables. The BBC contributed £1,000 and in the end the letter produced £17,000 in cash.

The Library now owed £20,000 to the Inland Revenue and legal fees. Geoffrey Lawrence nobly waived his fee of £700, and all we could do in gratitude was to make him an honorary life member of the Library.

Later in October I took my charming French author Maurice Druon to the Tower of London, and soon after that I made a speech to the Robert Louis Stevenson Society.

In November Comfort and I celebrated our silver wedding with a small dinner-party at the Garrick Club.

THE ![masthead crest] TIMES

Thursday November 5 1959

LONDON LIBRARY

Sir,—After a legal battle which has lasted more than three years and which culminated yesterday in an adverse decision by the Court of Appeal, the London Library finds itself called upon to pay rates of some £5,000 a year.   For 80 years the London Library had been wholly exempt from payment of rates, until 1957, when the Inland Revenue imposed this assessment against which our appeal has ended in failure.

In 1958 the library found itself obliged to raise subscriptions to 10 guineas—a substantial increase over the four guineas of 1950.   To find annually a sum of £5,000 in addition to our normal running expenses is itself a matter of grave concern to us. Nevertheless, with the help of authors, publishers, and other benefactors we hope to be able to carry this grievous burden in the future.   We are faced, however, with an immediate crisis.   Our rating liability dates from 1956 and our accrued debt for rates and legal costs amounts to more than £20,000—a debt which must be paid at once.

If we can obtain the reprieve which the settlement of our debt of £20,000 would give us, we shall proceed to build up an endowment fund so that we can continue our contribution to the literary and educational life of the country.   We cannot, in the space of this letter of appeal, rehearse the benefits which the London Library has conferred, or enlarge upon the disaster which its disappearance would bring upon the whole community: we hope that its vital importance to the nation is so generally recognized that we shall not have appealed in vain.

Cheques should be made payable to the London Library and sent to the Librarian at 14, St. James's Square, London, S.W.1. All donations will be most gratefully acknowledged.

Yours faithfully,

T. S. ELIOT, President; RUPERT HART-DAVIS, Chairman, The London Library.

14, St. James's Square, S.W.1.

Printed by THE TIMES PUBLISHING COMPANY, Limited. Printing House Square, London, E.C.4, England.

[5]

The new year opened with a bang. Christie's generously offered to hold a book and picture sale on behalf of the Library without charge. The Queen and the Queen Mother gave rare and valuable old books, and I spent most of the next five months busily cadging manuscripts, books and pictures from all the leading writers and artists that I knew.

My first visit was to E.M. Forster, whom I found sitting on the floor of his Cambridge sitting-room, surrounded by hundreds of sheets of paper. They were the original manuscript of his novel *A Passage to India* and he was struggling to put them in the right order. I told him I would do that for him, gathered them up, put them in my despatch-case and after warmly thanking him I bore them back to London. At the auction they fetched £6,500, which was then the highest sum ever paid for a modern English manuscript.

Lytton Strachey's brother James gave me the original manuscript and corrected proofs of Lytton's *Queen Victoria*, which fetched £1,800.

I visited John Masefield in his rather desolate-looking house by the Thames. His wife had died recently, and I found him sadly painting a beautiful little picture of a ship. He told me, bless him, that he had gathered together no fewer than *170* of his books and pamphlets, in each of which he had written a signed inscription referring to the Library. They fetched only £200, which I thought shamefully little.

Tom Eliot and his wife Valerie were just starting on a holiday in North Africa when I asked Tom if he could possibly give me the manuscript of his long poem 'The Waste Land' for the sale. He said he would gladly have done so if it hadn't been lost long ago.[1] I timidly asked him if he would write out the poem again, and he said certainly, so I bought some large sheets of excellent paper and a Penguin edition of the poem. Halfway through their holiday I had a postcard from Tom saying 'O Chairman, my Chairman, the fearful task is done'.[2] At

1 Years later it was found in America.
2 Cf. Walt Whitman's poem 'O Captain! my Captain!'

Maquette by Henry Moore

the sale it fetched £2,800 and everyone cheered. Tom beamed happily. Later he told me he had included in the transcript one line which he had accidentally omitted before. The American university which bought the transcript checked it line by line and were overjoyed to find the missing line.

And so the gifts flowed on – Byron letters from Harold Nicolson £600, Somerset Maugham's manuscript of his novel *Up at the Villa* £1,100, much T.E. Lawrence material from his brother Arnold £3,800, and lastly my favourite of all. I visited the great sculptor Henry Moore and he gave me a little carved bronze object about three feet long. I couldn't help asking him what it was, and it turned out to be maquette for a screen on the Time-Life building in Bond Street. It fetched £700. Altogether the sale, which was held on 22 June 1960, brought in £25,000, which, together with the £17,000 raised by our letter in *The Times*, came to much more than the Library's immediate needs.

Although the Christie's sale had occupied most of my time for the first half of 1960, there was much else going on. In February Jonathan Cape died, and I had to write his obituary for *The Times* and attend his funeral at Petersham near Richmond. In the same month I was chairman at the Foyle's Literary Lunch in honour of J.B. Priestley. By April the galley-proofs of the Oscar Wilde letters began to pour in; and Ruth and I checked and corrected them in a brief visit to Kisdon, and at the end of the month I opened the third Antiquarian Book Fair and happily met Yehudi Menuhin there. Another few days at Kisdon in May enabled us to deal with the next lot of galley-proofs, which we could seldom get time to do in London.

In July Ruth and I had the excitement of being the first people to see the original manuscript of Oscar's longest, best, and most important letter *De Profundis*, which had been given to the British Museum by Robbie Ross with a fifty-year ban on anyone's seeing it, so as to make sure Lord Alfred Douglas never saw it. To our delight we found that the published versions were wildly inaccurate, so our version in *The Letters* was the first accurate text in print.

Another short visit to Kisdon, and in November I travelled to Rapallo to represent Eva Reichmann at the unveiling of the plaque on the outside of Max's villino. I managed to correct a hundred pages of Oscar's letters on boat and train.

[6]

Early in 1961 Duff got a job at the birth of the *Sunday Telegraph*, and the galley-proofs of the Oscar Wilde letters were still flooding in from the printer.

In the last week of February Ruth and I set off for a business visit to New York on the *Queen Mary*. We stayed with friends and I was visiting and being entertained by countless publishers, editors and writers. It was Ruth's first visit to the United States and, as I foresaw, she was a *succès fou* with the gentlemen. Except for a weekend in

*New College,
Warden's Garden.
Back row: John
Julius Norwich,
Anthony Powell,
Peter Quennell.
Lower row: Sir
William Hayter,
R. H.-D.,
Raymond Mortimer*

Boston and Harvard we were all the time in New York, overwhelmed by the hospitality and friendliness of everyone. I didn't get any exciting books to publish, but I'm sure we gained a lot of good will instead. At the end of March we came home on the *Queen Elizabeth*, on board which in 1943 I had travelled home with 15,000 American servicemen.

The high spot of April was Duff's wedding to Phyllida Barstow in the depths of Wales. In the same month Comfort and I attended a luncheon in Merton College, Oxford, for the opening of the Max Beerbohm Room. And now the first page-proofs of Oscar letters began to arrive, and apart from correcting them I had to begin the enormous index, which took me six months to compile in my spare time and occupied eighty large double-column pages in the published volume.

At the end of July I spent a week in the Middlesex Hospital, undergoing every sort of painful and humiliating test for the cause of my abdominal pain, which was finally diagnosed as diverticulitis in the duodenum, which was cured by medicine and a strict diet.

On 17 August Adam flew to Delhi to spend a year of Voluntary Service Overseas teaching at a school in the Central Province of India. A week later Ruth and I set out for a fortnight's visit to her daughter at Forte dei Marmi on the Italian coast north of Viareggio. The climate was perfect and we spent most of our time on the beach and in the sea, from which there is a wonderful view of the Carrara mountains, black and white with green trees and little villages below them.

In October, after the success of Gerry Durrell's *My Family and Other Animals* I published 50,000 copies of his new book *The Whispering Land*, wishing that I had another author so prolific and regular.

Relations with Heinemann were now at breaking-point, and at the last moment a *deus ex machina* appeared on the scene. His name was Bill Jovanovich. His father was a Yugoslav peasant who managed to emigrate to the USA and got work in a Pittsburgh steelworks. He married a Polish girl who gave birth to Bill, who won every conceivable prize and scholarship, ending with a Ph.D. in Eng. Lit. By the time he was thirty-four he was president of Harcourt Brace, one of the leading US publishers of quality.

He apparently thought a lot of my firm, and would like to have a subsidiary firm in England. You would have thought that Heinemann should have been delighted to get rid of a money-losing subsidiary, but they seemed to think that selling anything to America was in some way selling the pass. In the end they gave way and the agreement with Harcourt Brace was signed in January 1962.

To add to my delight I had by the end of 1961 finished my index and correcting the proofs of the Oscar Wilde letters – the end of seven years of travail.

In December I flew to New York at Bill's request and flew home three days later. Once again the plane was diverted to Shannon Airport.

[7]

In January 1962 I journeyed to Edinburgh, stayed with Hugh Walpole's brother Robin and took him to the annual dinner of the Scottish Bookmen, to whom I made a speech.

Cheerful letters from Adam told of his visit to Kashmir and the Taj Mahal. And then, after a long illness, dear George Lyttelton died of cancer on 1 May. Ruth and I travelled sadly to his funeral at Grundisburgh. I felt lost without him, after our six years of weekly correspondence and meetings in London. He was a great man and I am mourning him to this day. Three weeks later, just too late for George to see the finished volume, *The Letters of Oscar Wilde* was published in 958 large pages on 25 June. George had read the proofs. When the first copies were printed and bound I discovered to my horror that if I didn't price them at four guineas I should lose money on every volume. In fact the first edition sold like hot cakes, and it became one of those books whose price doesn't matter. We were enjoying a three-week holiday on Kisdon, so the excellent reviews by Harold Nicolson, Tony Powell, Cyril Connolly and others reached us gradually day by day.

As soon as the agreement with Heinemann was signed Bill lost no time in getting things to work. He started by giving me a five-year contract at £4,000 a year, a sum beyond my wildest hopes, sent over his Education partner to arrange an education department for us, and hired some extra offices in Dean Street, behind Soho Square. But he infuriated me by saying that Ruth must leave the firm because she and I were living together. I told him I had never heard such nonsense, but he gave Ruth a golden handshake of £500 and that was that.

Altogether we published fifty-four books in 1962, including the first four of twelve volumes of Henry James's short stories, *The Marconi Scandal* by Frances Donaldson and *The Black Prince* by Maurice Druon.

[8]

Early in 1963 the crash came. Bill had been here in January and I've never known the cause of it, but I imagine that the shareholders of

Harcourt Brace must have refused to continue the loss of money caused by their English subsidiary. Bill could not oppose them. What he should have done was immediately to fly over here, as he had several times done, and discuss with me what could be done to resolve the matter. I can only attribute his failure in this to lack of moral courage. Instead, without a word to me, he sent over a junior editor with orders to sell our firm if possible, and if there were no takers, to liquidate it.

The poor young man had never been in England before and knew few English publishers. He spent most of his time in the Connaught Hotel with a bottle of whisky. As soon as the news of his arrival and orders was known in London, most of the publishers reacted violently, and several of them refused ever to deal with Harcourt Brace again.

To help and advise me I called on my old friend Arnold Goodman. Now he had his own firm Goodman Derrick, and I visited him in his office off Fleet Street. He asked me to tell him of my troubles and I spoke, quite fast, for ten or fifteen minutes, telling him every detail of my firm's existence from its initiation, with exact figures of capital, expenditure, sales, etc.

Arnold never interrupted me, but when I had finished he said: 'That's most interesting and we must have a record of it', rang for his secretary and dictated to her absolutely everything I'd said, mostly in my own words, but altering and omitting nothing – the most amazing feat of mental agility I've ever seen or heard of. When he had succeeded in persuading Granada Television to buy the business, to me he became a miracle man, and I wasn't surprised when he became a leading trouble-shooter for the government, Master of University College, Oxford, a baron, and a Companion of Honour. I only once had an opportunity to praise him and his work out loud in his presence, and that was at a luncheon given by W.H. Smith Ltd.

I never heard a word from Bill, but I couldn't resist sending him a letter saying: 'On one of my flights to New York at your behest I was shown into your office and you jumped to your feet, put your arms round me and embraced me. To your secretary, who looked somewhat startled, you said: "In Montenegro, where I come from, when a man greets another man like that it means that whatever happens he'll never let him down." Too bad we weren't in Montenegro at the time.'

But this disaster proved to be my liberation, for I was able to secure the unpaid three-fifths of my American contract. They amounted to £12,000, with which I was able to buy and rehabilitate the lovely old house in which I have lived for the rest of my life.

My interest in publishing had long since evaporated, my children and Ruth's were grown up and away from home, my promise to keep the family together had been carried out, and Comfort was quite prepared to divorce me.

Ruth and I became the guilty parties, and we were told a detective would come to see us to prove that we were living together at 36 Soho Square. On the appointed evening Ruth put on a dressing-gown to make it clear that she lived in the flat, as she did, and when the front-door bell rang at the arranged time I sped down the three floors, and was astonished to admit a good-looking middle-aged woman who said she was a detective. She came up and had drinks with us and told us a lot of interesting things about her work.

Thereafter Ruth and I lived mostly on our beloved Kisdon, whence I went up to London occasionally for the London Library, the Literary Society or the publishing business.

That year brought other blessings to my family. On 27 May Duff's lovely daughter Alice was born, and on 15 June our Bridget was married to David Trustram Eve in the Temple Church. On the eve of the wedding David's father, Malcolm Trustram Eve (later Lord Silsoe) and I went to the church to see it was all in order. As we were walking away across the quadrangle we ran into John Foster QC, whom we both knew. 'What are you both doing here?' he asked. 'Oh,' said Malcolm, 'Rupert and I are being married here tomorrow.' Foster walked on puzzled.

On 22 June Ruth and I were driving from Kisdon to Richmond on the top road with its magnificent views. As we approached the little village of Marske-in-Swaledale we saw a lovely eighteenth-century house on a green slope looking southward over the valley. It had a 'For sale' notice in a big window. We went up to the village post office and asked what the house was. 'Oh', said Mrs Wellburn, whom we came to know well, 'it's the Old Rectory. It's been empty for six years. Would you like the key?' 'Yes, please.'

We had long realised that, though Kisdon Lodge had been our heaven on earth for nine years, it was not a place to grow old in. No electricity or sanitation, and the only means of reaching the cottage up a rough hillside were in a Land Rover, tractor or on foot.

We eagerly examined all twenty-three rooms of the house, which were in a shocking state. Cows had got into the big drawing-room, and most of the other rooms were full of dead birds, peeling wallpaper and prayer-books, and there was a hole in the roof. It was all icy-cold, and we could see where the parsons had been driven into corners with oil-lamps.

The Old Rectory, with Horst Schroeder in foreground

View from the Old Rectory

We both fell in love with the house and its surroundings, and I immediately wrote to the Church Commissioners, asking whether they would sell the house to me. They wrote back to say that the Rectory didn't belong to them, but to the Ripon Diocesan Dilapidations Board at Leeds. I wrote to them, but they passed the buck back to the Church Commissioners. Luckily Malcolm Trustram Eve was on their board, so I wrote asking him to hurry things up before the house fell to pieces. They agreed to mend the hole in the roof at once.

Meanwhile a little orchard and rose-garden at the bottom of the short lane leading to the Rectory was coming up for auction. We longed to have it, and taking a chance on our getting the Rectory, we bid for the small garden and got it for £300.

[9]

I had streams of letters from the Church Commissioners and the Ripon Dilapidations Board, but it took more than six months for the house to be auctioned. This happened on 16 April 1964. Ruth was in bed with flu in London, so I travelled up to Richmond by train and in the King's Head succeeded in getting the house and the field in front of it for £4,200. If Mr Richardson of Darlington had not bid against me I should probably have got it for half as much.

We immediately set about repairing the house and arranged for Gordon Walker from Reeth to install central-heating radiators in every room. He eventually installed twenty-nine. We also got in touch with our old friend Percy Calvert at Gunnerside, who had put Kisdon Lodge in order for us, and asked him to do the same for the Rectory, which he did with great skill and an admirable team of men. One masterly young carpenter made and fixed many miles of movable bookshelves all over the house.

We stayed mostly at Kisdon and drove over every day to see how everything was getting on. They always seemed to work more quickly when we were there. On 19 May we went round with Calvert's men, positioning sockets, switches, lights and radiators in every room. One day we skipped our morning visit to find that the wallpaper in one of the bathrooms had been put on upside down, which it still is.

In May we bought three fenders at a sale at Ronaldkirk. We kept two for ourselves and gave one to Bobbie, who said it was just what he wanted for his new manure-spreader.

On 13 June Bridget's daughter Amy was born.

Meanwhile Comfort had got a decree nisi divorce, which became absolute on 14 October 1964. Five days later Ruth and I came up to London and were married, after eighteen years of longing, at Caxton Hall on 19 October. Hans and Eva Reichmann had promised to be our witnesses, but, alas, Hans had died, so dear Eva came alone, bringing presents, as did Alistair Cooke's wife Jane and my lawyer Robert Keeling. The officiator was a charming man called Mr Digweed.

Our brief honeymoon was spent happily at Prestonfield House on the
outskirts of Edinburgh. It is a lovely old building which had been in the
possession of the Dick family as a private house for generations. Among
its visitors were Bonnie Prince Charlie, Boswell and Doctor Johnson,
and the house still looked and felt much more like a private house than
any hotel I've ever seen: there was delicious food and a fine old bar
selling every known brand of malt whisky, a comfortable bedroom with
a lovely view over a loch to Arthur's Seat. We made friends with Janet
Dick-Cunnyngham, the owner/manager. We left after four comfortable nights, our breakfast brought up to us in bed and immensely
delicious meals. Total bill £32. We walked all round Edinburgh,
admiring her, and in Thin's bookshop I bought good first editions
of Stevenson's *Child's Garden of Verses* and Scott's *Quentin Durward*.

Directly we got back to Yorkshire we wrote to the Church
Commissioners yet again, this time to ask them to sell us the field
behind the house. After some delay they wrote to say that we should
need a faculty to deconsecrate the path between the gate and the new
churchyard, which occupies the far corner of the field. I wrote back
to say there was no path and never had been. It was all green field.
After another pause I received a letter saying that we should need
another faculty to enable us to step over the path. This was getting
like the Mad Hatter in *Alice in Wonderland*, so I wrote again to the
Commissioners, who immediately agreed to sell us the field for £300,
on condition that no chickens were allowed on it. We had no
intention of having chickens anywhere, but I couldn't resist asking
why not. Because, they said, they might fly over the fence and dig up
the graves. I told them that most people were buried six foot down,
and the pecking-power of chickens was a few inches. After this
charade my respect for the Church of England was considerably
reduced, but we went to church every Sunday and I read the lessons.

By now the hot water supply in the Rectory was in full flow and on
24 October we spent our first night here. Three days later we sadly
left Kisdon Lodge for the last time, almost in tears, and Ruth kissed
the doorpost as I locked the door. I have never been back there. That
night was our first at the Rectory, in the only bedroom that was

completely furnished. Just before we were going to turn off the bedside light at 10 p.m. the whole of the village's electricity collapsed. We took this to be a welcome for our arrival.

Between then and the end of the year furniture and other things arrived – from the Walpole house in Corstorphine, Ruth's house in Hampstead, the flat and office in Soho Square, Kisdon Lodge and Bromsden Farm, where the books filled one hundred and ninety-seven tea-chests. All, or most, of this was dumped in the big drawing-room, which was to be the last room painted and decorated.

The room had a horrid little fireplace, and while we were wondering where we could get a suitable one, Peter Leech, who was living in Marske Lodge, the nearest house to the Rectory, told us he had just removed a fireplace to make room for a deep freeze. We went to see it, thought it exactly what we wanted and asked Peter if he would sell it to us. He said yes, but he'd ask an expert what it was worth. A few days later he told us rather shamefacedly that the expert said £30. We agreed to pay that, but Peter relieved his conscience by throwing in the kitchen table, 6 foot by 3 foot 6, which has staunchly carried food and drink to us and our guests for more than thirty years.

Meanwhile the whole of the rest of the house was busy with carpenters, masons, electricians, painters, plumbers and goodness knows who else. On 10 December I counted seventeen workers hard at it. Lorry-loads of rubbish were removed, including sixty empty wine-bottles hidden away in what had been the outside privy. Clearly the parsons had been shy about disclosing empties. Percy Calvert persuaded some good women from Keld to come and scrub all the floors in the house.

That autumn we made friends with two of the nicest people I've ever known, Boyk and Nellie Severs. Boyk was a farm-hand when we met him, and he offered to build and repair the stone walls round our land, a task at which he was expert. Nell (as we always called her) came and worked regularly in the house. Then Boyk got a job as warden of the army range at the top of the hill behind Marske. He had a hut to sit in, and his only jobs were to put up red flags when they were firing on the range and generally look after the area. He became very interested in gardening, and we subscribed to a paper

Boyk and Nellie Severs

called *Amateur Gardening*, which Boyk read from cover to cover in his hut. Then in his spare time he gardened for us for years.

On 28 November 1964 Duff's son Guy was born and the year ended happily for us in our new home.

[10]

We received the saddest news at the beginning of 1965. Early in the morning of 5 January the radio told us that T.S. Eliot had died the day before. As a result of our companionship in the London Library and its troubles Ruth and I had become very fond of Tom and his beloved wife Valerie. Later in the morning the *Sunday Telegraph* asked me to write a personal memoir of Tom in 650 words. This I did in two days, then dictated it all to the paper on the telephone and it duly appeared there on Sunday 10 January.

Earlier, four days after Eliot's death, this poem was published in *The Times*:

'East Coker'

Here, whence his forebears sprang, a man is laid
As dust, in quiet earth, whose written word
Helped many thousands broken and dismayed
Among the ruins of triumphant wrong.
May many an English flower and little bird
(Primrose and robin redbreast unafraid)
Gladden this garden where his rest is made
And Christmas song respond, and Easter song.[1]

JOHN MASEFIELD

A month later we went up to London to attend his memorial service in Westminster Abbey, in which Alec Guinness read beautifully. The death of Winston Churchill on 24 January was the end of an epoch.

By this time the last of the bookshelves in the library were in place, and I happily began to unpack and arrange some of the books, and we planted 250 daffodils in the orchard. As soon as sufficient bedrooms and bathrooms were finished the flood of visitors began with Janet Stone, who was followed by Alistair and Jane Cooke. Everyone who stayed the night was obliged to sign the visitors' book, and to my astonishment I find that in this dawn of our life in the Rectory (1965) there were fifty-nine signatures in the book. Twelve of them were of members of my family who came several times, but heading the list were Andrew Young, Janet Adam Smith (whom we always called Danny, which was what she had called herself when she was a little girl), Leon Edel, Hugh Wheeler, Geoffrey Keynes, Peggy Ashcroft, Peter Fleming and Richard Garnett.

Luckily Nell came to work regularly and very efficiently all over the inside of the house. Marske had a charming vicar called Arthur Cave, who was vicar of two other small parishes. Very early in our friendship he asked me if I would join a committee which was just

1 Reprinted by permission of the Society of Authors.

being formed in an attempt to turn the deserted Marrick Priory into an adventure centre. I attended the first meeting in Richmond Town Hall. The chairman was the Archdeacon of Ripon, a charming old man who was always anxious to postpone everything to the next meeting. Years later, when he retired I succeeded him as chairman. And the Adventure Centre still flourishes today.

An old friend Nancy Crathorne (née Tennant), who lived not far away, had just rescued the eighteenth-century Georgian Theatre in Richmond from the indignity of having been for a long time a repository of rubbish. Luckily all the original stalls and boxes were still in place. Directly Nancy heard that I was living near Richmond she asked me to join the theatre committee, assuring me that I should have very little to do. This proved to be true, because Nancy did everything, but when she died suddenly I was persuaded to take her place, which I reluctantly did. Somehow I managed to persuade friends to come and stay with us to give solo performances in the theatre – Joyce Grenfell, Edith Evans, Marie Rambert, Micheál Mac Liammóir, Emlyn Williams.

On 28 September I gave an address on T.S. Eliot in the village church of East Coker, near Taunton in Somerset. It was his memorial service and the burying of his ashes in the church. I had never spoken from a pulpit before, but directly I got into it I realised what a powerful position it is, and my words were approved by Valerie. My address was reprinted in my book *Praise from the Past* (1996).

One day I went up to London for a Literary Society dinner. I was washing my hands in the Garrick Club washroom, when Tommy Lascelles[1] and Siegfried Sassoon came in. Tommy said: 'Siegfried and I have been talking in the taxi and we've come to the conclusion that it's high time you were knighted. Have you any objection?' I said: 'I've no objection – but I never thought of such a thing.' 'Leave it to me', said Tommy.

---

1 Sir Alan (always called Tommy) Lascelles, a courtier who had been private secretary to four English monarchs.

Most of October was spent on organising the inside of the house and the garden. We drove all round the countryside looking for unwanted flagstones for our terrace and paths.

My diary for the end of the year records: in November a meeting at Marrick Priory with architects, etc. Our first heavy snowfall. Micheál Mac Liammóir with his friend and helper Brian Tobin came to stay, heralded by a telegram from Dublin reading 'ARRIVING TODAY GOD HELP YOU ALL LOVE MICHEÁL', to perform his Oscar Wilde narrative which he called *The Importance of Being Oscar* in the Georgian Theatre. Then after he had gone, snow a foot deep. Planted mahonia at the end of the terrace, where it flourishes to this day. Drove to York University and made friends with Professor Norman, and in the Richmond Convent made great friends with Mother Margaret Mary. After Christmas Peter Fleming arrived with a brace of pheasants and another of black game.

Ruth in her new home

Peter Fleming

[11]

All through 1966 we were as happy and busy as before in the house, where Ruth made curtains for all thirty-one windows and I unpacked books and worked away at my large *Catalogue of the Caricatures of Max Beerbohm*, which eventually appeared in 1972. And outside we had a greenhouse built, which Boyk was now painting white. He was also laying flagstone paths all round the place, and we weeded and bonfired a great deal of rubbish.

One morning we woke to the sound of chain-saws very near us. We dressed hastily and ran down to the acre of woodland on both sides of Marske Beck, where all the trees on the far bank had been felled except for a few small yews and a magnificent huge sycamore, on which chains were already fixed ready for felling. We stopped the workers and asked who they were. They said they were working for a timber-merchant who had bought the acre long ago. We asked them to spare the sycamore and said we would buy the acre, which we did for £300, and the sycamore still reigns supreme.

On 17 April Bridget's son Simon was born. In June Marie Rambert came for two nights and put on two charming programmes of teaching little girls ballet-dancing on the Georgian Theatre's tiny stage. Marie was a Polish dancer who had performed with Nijinsky in the Diaghilev Ballet. She was married to the playwright Ashley Dukes and I had met her in 1929 when Peg had her first London success in Ashley's adaptation of Leon Feuchtwanger's long novel *Jew Süss*. Now she was running her own Ballet Rambert, based at the Mercury Theatre in London but travelling all over the country.

When we met at Darlington station in 1966, she said: 'How nice to find you again. I see you've grown a moustache. So have I.' When we got home I asked her if she would like to lie down for a while before lunch. 'No, no,' she said. 'I'll just stand on my head for a little and then I'll be quite all right.' She was a delicious guest.

Late in November I found that Tommy Lascelles had been as good as his word, when I received from the Prime Minister's Principal Private Secretary a letter headed 'Honours In Confidence', in which I was told that I was on the list for a knighthood in the New Year Honours 1967. There was a list of the travelling and other expenses which would be paid if necessary. We decided to tell nobody about this honour until it was announced on New Year's Day.

Among fifty-eight other guests in 1966 were Tommy Lascelles, Reynolds Stone, Joyce and Reggie Grenfell, Diana Cooper, Andrew Young, Eva Reichmann and my cousin John Julius Norwich.

[12]

Sunday 1 January 1967: knighthood reported in every paper and the telephone rang all day. The first ringer was Peg. During the next few days the postman reeled in with some four hundred letters, many of which were so kind and generous that I felt I must answer them. We had asked Boyk and Nell to come down for a drink at eleven. (They lived in a cottage just beyond our top field.) When they arrived we showed them my name in the *Sunday Times*. Boyk was thrilled, shook hands with me and congratulated me very correctly. After lunch when we went out of the back door we found a paper bag containing a few potatoes, onions and other vegetables. Boyk and Nell felt that a present was in order and gave us all they had to give. We were deeply touched.

Next day the village farmer Ronnie Simpson brought us a load of manure for the garden, saying my knighthood was an honour to the village and everyone in his house was delighted. Mrs Wellburn kept coming down with telegrams and was overcome by excitement.

On January 16 and 17 we spent the nights at Prestonfield House and in between went to Compton (Monty) Mackenzie's eighty-fourth birthday party: charming people and an excellent supper. Someone made a good moving speech and Monty made a better and more moving answer. Soon after we got home Bobbie and Ivy rang up from Keld. They had been too shy to ring before, they said, and didn't know what to say. We drove over to see them next day. They were as sweet as ever, but it was clear that they would always call us Mr and Mrs Davis!

We spent two days in January in London buying suitable clothes for Buckingham Palace, where we were due to appear on 7 February.

On 31 January we drove to Darlington and took the train to Edinburgh, where we were to attend Tim Devlin's wedding. We had a carriage to ourselves, and when we had nearly reached our destination Ruth went along the corridor to tidy herself up. When she came back, looking very trim and beautiful, I was correcting someone's proofs, and Ruth said: 'What a distinguished-looking husband I've got.' I laughed that off and gave her a kiss, little knowing that those were almost her last words.

The train was late, and I said we must hurry to catch a cab, to avoid missing the wedding. We couldn't run because of the crowd, but we walked as fast as we could, and caught a taxi. As it was driving up the little incline from the station Ruth said: 'Have you told him where to go?' I said 'Yes, darling.' Then she gave two loud choking noises and collapsed into my arms. I instinctively knew she was dead, but I just hugged her and told the driver to get to the infirmary as quickly as possible.

For some years Ruth had had a heart murmur and every year she went to a heart-specialist, who listened to her heart and tested her blood-pressure, always telling her it was no worse than the year before.

They carried her out and left me in the waiting-room. Soon they came and told me she was dead. I was so stunned by the blow that I didn't know what to do or say, until I telephoned to the place where the Devlin wedding reception was taking place and told Tim's mother Madeleine what had happened. She, bless her, came straight to the infirmary to hold my hand. In my state of shock I started to worry about our car, which we had left in an unauthorised place outside Darlington station. They told me I should have to come back next morning, in case there had to be an inquest, so I went into the room where Ruth was lying, kissed her on the forehead and staggered away in tears.

Waiting at the station I had several large whiskies, hoping they would steady me up. In the train I was in a carriage along with an agreeable man, who asked me if I was in trouble, whereupon I poured out the whole story of the day to him. He was most sympathetic, and turned out to be a friend of my son Duff, to whom he said he would telephone as soon as he got home.

I found the car safely at Darlington, and as I drove slowly home I thought I should never get to sleep without a powerful soporific, so I stopped at Dr Mac's house in Richmond and rang the bell. The door was opened by Mrs Mac, who was said to have second sight. She immediately said 'I knew you were coming', and went to get a sleeping draught from Dr Mac. Nothing in the whole day seemed real.

Next morning I returned to Edinburgh in the train we had so happily journeyed in the previous day. They told me there was no question of an inquest, so I just made arrangements for Ruth to be brought to Marske for burial, and then went back home. My sister Deirdre came to look after me.

The funeral took place on 4 February, and she was laid to rest in the burial ground in the corner of our top field. Later I got dear Reynolds Stone to carve a headstone for the grave, at the foot of which I included Tennyson's words

> Death has made
> His darkness beautiful with thee.

It was only three days before I was due at Buckingham Palace for the investiture. Although I was feeling half-alive I thought it was best to get through it now, rather than have it hanging over me. So Deirdre and I travelled to London and spent two nights in the home in Dean's Yard of Danny and her husband John Carleton, the headmaster of Westminster School. On 7 February I went to the Palace with Deirdre and Duff. When we got there I and the other candidates had to stand about for almost three-quarters of an hour, repeatedly being told how to get down on one knee and how to get up again. I was saved from desperation by my dear old friend Neville Cardus, the cricket writer, who was in the same situation as I was. He said 'I can't go through all this again. You can't sit down, you can't get a drink and you can't spend a penny. I did it all when I got my CBE, and if they offer me a life-peerage I shall turn it down.'

The Queen looked very young and pretty in a gay cocktail dress. I couldn't help thinking that when she tapped the shoulder of a kneeling man with a sword and turned him into a Knight Bachelor she should have worn an impressively royal dress. I longed to know whether she would say 'Rise, Sir Rupert' or 'Arise, Sir Rupert', but in fact Her Majesty spoke no word.

PART THREE: HALFWAY TO HEAVEN

Idle and light are many things you see
In these my closing pages. Blame not me.
However rich and plenteous the repast
Nuts, almonds, biscuits, wafers come at last.

LANDOR

Thy thoughts and feelings shall not die,
Nor leave thee when grey hairs are nigh,
A melancholy slave;
But an old age, alive and bright,
And lovely as a Lapland night,
Shall lead thee to thy grave.

WORDSWORTH

[1]

TWO MONTHS BEFORE Ruth's death she had a brilliant idea. She was overwhelmed with typing answers to letters and a lot of my literary work. We had always kept in touch with my long-lost secretary June. Her husband had died in 1964 and since then she had been secretary to the Warden (headmaster) of Radley College. Ruth wrote to her there, asking if she could possibly come up to help during the Easter holidays. June wrote back to say she would love to come. In hindsight it seems as though the whole thing had been *meant*.

When Ruth died June sent me a lovely letter of condolence and I wrote back, saying I hoped she would still come to help, since I needed her more than ever because, apart from my usual load of typing, I now had another four hundred letters to answer. The most moving of them was from Siegfried Sassoon:

Heytesbury House
21.2.67

Dear Dear Rupert

It is a great relief to my mind that I *can* now write to you, as I have felt utterly helpless in my continuous sharing of your desolation, and could only say over and over again – 'how *can* he go on?' – what *can* I do to help him? I don't know when a friend's bereavement has caused me such poignant and prolonged distress. This is all I have to offer you. Every word in your grievous letter had already been in my mind, day in, day out, since Feb. 9th (when the shock stunned me in a letter from Hester – I, who had been picturing you and darling Ruth at the Investiture). The thought of you alone up there has been almost unbearable. I loved Ruth at first sight, and the thought of you two together had been an abiding happiness in my solitude.

Dear Rupert, you have shared the bereavements of others in your noble heart; and you know that we just *have* to go on somehow. And Ruth would tell you that you *must*, though your ideal companionship has been so cruelly destroyed at a single blow. One thing I *can* offer you – my deep and devoted friendship, for you have come to be – though I see you so seldom – a source of strength and encourage-ment beyond anyone else, except Mother Margaret Mary, so few of my closest friends being left to me now. I beg you to turn toward me for solace, reduced though I am in energy and activity. There is nothing I wouldn't do to redeem your desolation.

And in *material* concerns I do need you, as I need no one else. All my future arrangements about literary remains etc. have come to depend on your incomparable ability to organise such things. Might it be a help, later on, if you were to come here and go through things with me? In my misery I have sometimes said to myself – 'I *shall* hear Rupert laugh that great laugh again – I shall'. And I firmly believe that her blessed spirit is with you, and that her love watches over you as always. Please, please try to believe this, though the mystery of undeserved suffering is the great problem of life and religion.

Ever yours Siegfried[1]

[2]

Meanwhile a string of loving ladies came to look after me, each for a few days – Deirdre, Bridget, Peg, Janet Stone, Danny, Joyce Grenfell and others. Often I went across the field to Boyk and Nell for supper and watched their television.

In February I went up to London for the day – a meeting in the office, tea with Eva Reichmann and home with Deirdre, who stayed a week. In March Peg came to look after me, and we got along as well as we did forty years ago. Peter Leech agreed to sell me the cottage which was attached to his house, and long ago had been the servants' quarters. I paid him £2,100 for it and began to have it put in order, so that I could install a married couple to look after me. I spent a good deal of time helping Boyk in the garden and doing a lot of literary work indoors.

I took Peg to see Middleham and Jervaulx Abbey, also Barnard Castle and the Bowes Museum. She was succeeded by Bridget, who cooked excellently and did a lot of work in the garden. Then Janet Stone took over. All these girls cooked for me, and left ready-cooked dishes when they departed.

When I was alone I wrote in my diary: 'Much comforted by speaking to Deirdre every evening. Otherwise desolation.' Joyce and Reggie came at the beginning of April. Boyk had flattened what was going to be the front lawn with spade and wheelbarrow. When Bridget was here she kept on telling him where there were dips in the surface, and in April I bought thirty pounds of lawn-seed.

---

1 I received more than thirty letters from Siegfried over the years, and, except for this one, all were signed by one capital S intertwined with another, as he signed most letters to other people. His signing this letter Siegfried shows that it came from his heart.

With June in the library

On 11 April I went up to London for the London Library and Literary Society, and stayed at Peg's house in Hampstead. Next day June arrived. She left Radley mid-morning, never having been further north than Cheltenham, by bus to Oxford, where she inadvertently took a ticket to Doncaster. When the train, after stopping at every station, got to Sheffield, there was another train on the other side of the platform, from which the guard shouted 'Change here for Doncaster!' June got out with her luggage, and only just in time realised that it was Darlington she was going to, so stepped back into the same train! The ticket-collector at Darlington was friendly. June then took an expensive taxi to Marske and at about 8 p.m. she nervously rang the front-door bell. I gave her a good drink and supper and sent her to bed.

Almost immediately we realised that we were in love with each other. I had always found her very attractive when she was my business secretary all those years ago, but while Ruth was alive I never made advances to any other woman.

When June left after five days I wrote her a letter every day until I saw her again. Directly she had left I wrote: 'In these five extraordinary days you have brought me from death to life, from despair to hope, from desolation to renewal.' Today those words may sound somewhat extravagant, but they were simply the truth. Every day she was away I wrote her a letter and every day she answered. Both lots of letters have been preserved and are very moving to read. I telephoned to her every day, sometimes twice. I couldn't resist sending her Siegfried Sassoon's lovely poem:

> What you are I cannot say;
> Only this I know full well –
> When I touched your face to-day
> Drifts of blossom flushed and fell.
>
> Whence you came I cannot tell;
> Only – with your joy you start
> Chime on chime from bell to bell
> In the cloisters of my heart.

On 22 April I drove to Droitwich to visit Comfort's darling step-mother in an old people's home, then on to Alveston near Stratford where I stayed with Peg. She took me to see *Coriolanus*, which I found too long and boring to keep me awake. Next day I attended Peg's Shakespeare recital with John Gielgud, Paul Schofield, Dorothy Tutin and others. Then I drove to Sussex, visited William Plomer at Hassocks and went on to stay with Deirdre in her house at Iford. Next day I reached Radley, where I picked June up and we had a sunny and loving picnic in a thicket. Left her at 3 and got home at 8, having driven 798 miles in those few days. Deirdre had given me a winter jasmine plant, which Boyk and I planted on the north wall of the house, where it is still flourishing after thirty years. Then came the great day when, after all the levelling and weeding, Boyk sowed grass on the front lawn.

June's mother, always called Mumsy, had her seventieth birthday, and although I'd never seen her I sent her a very large bunch of flowers.

At the beginning of May I spent a peaceful weekend with my old and dear friend Wyndham Ketton-Cremer in his lovely house Felbrigg near Norwich, and later in the month Benjamin Britten and Peter Pears came to Richmond and gave a delightful performance at the Georgian Theatre, after which we socialised. The following day June came up for

Joyce and Reggie by the beck

three nights, and cooked us an excellent lunch on the Sunday. Duff came up for a week and did a great deal of work in the garden.

I had more visits from Danny, and from Joyce and Reggie – all lovely people. Arthur Ransome died on 3 June after many months in a nursing home. Now I quote from my diary:

6–9 June. I stayed with Siegfried Sassoon at Heytesbury.

10 June. I drove to Radley and picked up June. Tea in Bath, on to the Royal Hotel at Weston-super-Mare, where we stayed for two thrilling nights. Lovely sunny days, during which we saw a miniature zoo on the promenade and I taught June how to do crosswords on a hot and sunny beach.

13 June. Day in London. Library and Literary Society. Stayed the night with Danny and John in Dean's Yard.

14 June. Home again to find Bridget and her children waiting for me. Boyk in bed with some heart trouble. He was taken to Scorton Hospital and I drove Nell over there every day to see him. She gave us excellent lunches in their cottage.

12 July.   Gave address at Ransome Memorial Service in St Martin-in-the-Fields.

23 July.   Boyk came home from hospital, but was house-bound for some time. To Didcot by train from London. Met there by June who put me up for the night. Next day drove her from Radley to Marske in her tiny car, packed with her belongings. Finished putting together a new edition of Siegfried's *War Poems* with the poet's approval, but while Boyk was in hospital I had to do all the mowing and other gardening, now greatly helped by June.

7 August.   Diana Cooper came for the night. Next day Brownlee Kirkpatrick came for three days to work on the Blunden bibliography.

9 August.   June's birthday. Took her and Brownlee to Bolton Castle for lunch.

22 August.   I had an SOS call from Siegfried and hastened to Heytesbury, where I found him in bed and he told me he was dying. He asked me to write to six of his best friends to save them from the shock. 'But', he said, 'don't write to Dennis Silk. He's leading a cricket side in Canada and I don't want to spoil his tour.' I spent the best part of two days with him, and then said a tearful farewell.

Edmund Blunden, Siegfried Sassoon and Dennis Silk

1 September.   Siegfried died.

6 September.   Siegfried's funeral and burial at Mells. Attended with Angela Baddeley.

[3]

Soon after Ruth's death I promised her daughter Jill that I would visit her in Italy in the summer. Now, although I had June with me for good, I felt I must keep that promise. I was at Forte dei Marni from 8 to 22 August. I stayed most comfortably at the Pensione Edelweiss, where there was splendid food and drink, and spent most of my time on the beach with Jill and her two little daughters, Louisa and Sophie.

There was an excellent sweet-shop in the town called *Principe*, where we took the children every day. When I was in sole charge of them on the beach and they became obstreperous I used the only three Italian words I knew – *Domani niente Principe* – which quelled them instantly.

On 18 August Adam's son Damon was born.

On 23 September June met me, apparently the only passenger on the train, at pitch-dark Radley station at 9.45 p.m.

Next day we drove to Heytesbury and went through Siegfried's diaries and other papers with his son George. Lunch there. Then on to Marlborough for tea with Dennis Silk.

September 25 was a gloriously happy day on which I drove June away from Radley for good, her car stuffed with the last of her possessions. Home at 6 p.m. Everything in splendid order. I should have wilted at the seventy-nine letters that were waiting for me, if I hadn't at last got June's help and lovely presence for ever.

The first days of our thirty years of happiness were peacefully spent at home. I dictated and June valiantly typed replies to the enormous number of unanswered letters, while I began to get back to my literary work. In between we gardened and shopped in Richmond. Boyk was up on his feet but able to do light work only.

We were delighted to hear that the Carnegie Foundation was giving £7,000 to Marrick Priory so that our plans for it could advance.

June was rather nervous at the thought of all the visitors who were expected. I tried to cut down the number and she took them all in her tiny stride.

On 10 October we went up to London and lunched with Deirdre. Then June went to stay with her friend Pamela Bright. Next day I went to Siegfried's memorial service in Cheyne Row and sat next to Edmund Blunden. I attended a Royal Literary Fund meeting, and spent a second night with Danny and John in Dean's Yard, followed by the Annual General Meeting of the London Library. Met June again at 6 p.m. at Kings Cross and went happily home together.

On 24 October Boyk was told he could get back to work.

I was now working steadily on my *Catalogue of Max Beerbohm's Caricatures*, which wasn't finished for another five years.

On 28 October the last of June's furniture arrived. During my occasional days in London I managed to see many of Max's drawings – a great help for my catalogue. On 31 December 1967 I wrote: 'Lovely cosy ending to this endless year.'

[4]

As the beginning of 1968 I was working on Max Beerbohm's dramatic criticism from his twelve years on the *Saturday Review*. He had chosen two volumes-worth called *Around Theatres*, but my dear friend Allan Wade had copied out all the rest of the articles, and I had his admirably accurate typescripts, which I published as *More Theatres* and *Last Theatres* in 1969 and 1970.

On 7 January I noted in my diary: 'Desk clear for first time in over a year', which shows what a wonderful help June was.

I went up to London once a month, to visit the office and attend the London Library meeting and Literary Society dinner, which I arranged for the same day. At the end of January Duff came and told us all about Ascension Island, about which he was writing a book.

The newly-weds

On 31 January, a year since my darling Ruth died, I felt very weepy and low. June was unbelievably angelic.

In April Boyk planted beside the beck three poplars, three pussy willows, one lilac and six maples. The new wood grew steadily as one of our neighbours gave us a chestnut tree and Joyce and Reggie Grenfell a splendid whitebeam – all in memory of Ruth.

Meanwhile June went to stay for a few days with Mumsy and then brought her here for her first visit. When I saw them get out of the train at Darlington my first surprise was that Mumsy was several inches lower than June's five foot! I had never seen Mumsy before but as soon as I reached them I flung my arms round her and gave her a hearty kiss, which clearly pleased her.

Two days later I went to London for my usual meetings and spent the night with Tommy Lascelles in the Old Stables of Kensington Palace.

During her visit Mumsy cleaned the oven – it took her half a day! She also did a lot of gardening with June. We took Mumsy to the gardens at Harlow Car and bought rock-plants in crowded tents.

One day at lunch she asked me 'Are you going to marry June, or are you not?' I said 'Yes, Mumsy, I am, in June.' Two days after Mumsy went home I spent a day in London, during which I bought a knife-rack for her.

I now quote my diary once more:

5 May.   June was confirmed in Marske church with a lot of children by the Bishop of Knaresborough, followed by a bun-fight in the village hall.

24 May.   Joyce and Reggie came to stay. Next day we all walked up the hill and back by the beck. Joyce collected forty-eight different wildflowers.

6 June.   Bought two broken garden-urns at a sale at Bedale. When we took them home we asked Boyk if he could mend them. 'Aye', he said, 'I'll fettle 'em up for ye', and they have been full of flowers on the terrace ever since.

13 June.   Married to my beloved June at 10.30 a.m. in Swale House, Richmond. Mr Graham officiated. We took Boyk and Nell as our witnesses, and as we drove back to Marske in hot sun Boyk said, 'It's a grand day, even if you're not getting married or owt.' Arthur Cave had prepared a little service and a blessing for us in our church. As we came out Boyk flung his arms round June, gave her a smacking kiss and cried out 'LADY June'.

Then we drank champagne on the terrace. Boyk, who had never tasted wine before, swilled off his glass and said: 'It's an acquired taste.' We wondered how he knew that phrase, but he drank his second glass. After our honeymoon we learnt that Nell wouldn't do anything in the afternoon but just 'sat laffin'. Boyk was so worried that he called in their next-door neighbour Evelyn Hill, who was a trained nurse. She took one look at Nell and said: 'She's tight.'

Meanwhile we drove north, having a lunch of sandwiches and shandy at Middleton-in-Teesdale and a full tea in the garden of a pub at Crocketford. At 5 p.m. we arrived at the Murray Arms Hotel at Gatehouse of Fleet. They told us they only had one bed vacant and apologised that it was in the Garden House. It consisted of a bedroom and bathroom in a little cottage with a garden, across the road from the hotel. We were very happy there. Champagne cocktails and a good dinner sent us to bed, drunk with sun, joy, and champagne.

Next day was even hotter and sunnier. We wrote letters in the hotel garden, then, taking a packed lunch from the hotel (which did us for lunch and tea), we drove to the beach at a little bay, where we camped on grass between rocks. Bathed twice and both got a little sunburnt. Then in the evening back to the hotel for a bath, followed by more champagne cocktails and another good dinner. No honeymoon could have had a happier or lovelier beginning.

The wonderful weather continued next day, as we sadly left Gatehouse and drove north. We lunched in the car by Loch Trool, then visited Culzean Castle, much enjoying its round drawing-room and staircase on the very edge of the sea. On to Troon where we took a very expensive bedroom in the Marine Hotel, walked on the golf-course after dinner and slept quite well despite the roar of planes homing in to nearby Prestwick.

Then came a lazy day on the beach at Largs; we slept in a nearby hotel. Next morning we drove the car on to the ferry at Ardrossan. Tea and baps on board, as Arran emerged mysteriously lovely from the mist. After landing we drove across the island to the Lagg Hotel, said to be the best in the island. Unfortunately they were full up, so we drove back to the capital, Brodick, and booked a room in the Douglas Hotel.

After lunch we drove along the coast to Whiting Bay, where we examined every inch of Cooper Angus Lodge and its gardens, which had been given to my Cooper grandparents by the 12th Duke of Hamilton, who then owned all the Isle of Arran. He was also Earl of Angus, hence the house's title. My mother spent all her childish holidays there, but, alas, the house was now a ruin, shortly to be demolished. The gardener's house, called Duff Cottage, was still being lived in.

Farewell to Cooper Angus Lodge

By this time we had both fallen in love with Arran, and as we drove round the whole island our delight increased. We could only stay there for a week, but every day was full of sun and birds of every kind. We went round Brodick Castle, with a tea-shop downstairs. On the terrace outside the chaffinches were so tame that they came and ate on our table.

After a week we drove sadly on to the ferry, watched the lovely Arran coastline disappear, and vowed we'd return next year. On the way south we stopped in a sandpit, where June went to sleep on my lap and I watched sand-martins bringing food to their young. We reached Gatehouse of Fleet in the evening, were given a nice bedroom in an annexe, and had champagne, an excellent dinner and Drambuie.

Whenever we drove through a town we stopped at a bookshop and in Dumfries I bought three books for five shillings. As we neared home and came over the top of a hill to get a fine view of Swaledale, June said: 'It takes a lot of beating.' Our brief but perfect honeymoon was over.

[5]

On 16 July we drove to my old home Bromsden Farm and saw Comfort and some of the children, drove on from there to Mumsy's bungalow at Walkford, near Bournemouth, and saw all June's family.

On 3 August I made a speech in a green field at the opening of the Reeth Church fête. June was given a bouquet and I a button-hole. Danny and John came for two nights; Leon Edel and his wife came for a brief visit. Boyk came and worked in the garden every day, helped by both of us. Peter Fleming looked in and gave us a brace of grouse. Whenever there was a Test Match we listened to it on the radio.

Boyk told us that on the ranges the army tanks were knocking down some of the stone walls, and we badly needed a lot of stones to finish the walls round our fields. Boyk was a first-class stone-waller. I wrote to the Army Land Agent and drove him up to look at the damaged walls. After some discussion he said that for £25 we could take away as many stones as we liked. Accordingly we bought a Land Rover for £50 and used it to collect load after load of stone. Boyk

Joyce, Boyk and Nell with us

loved driving it, especially over rough ground, and he knew exactly which stones to take, the rectangular ones with no round sides. When we had collected as many stones as we wanted we sold the Land Rover back to the people we bought it from for £50.

At the end of August my friend John Stewart (who had written many crime novels as Michael Innes and a few straight ones as J.I.M. Stewart) wrote asking me if I would join him in a two-man viva in his college, Christ Church, Oxford, where he was a lecturer in English. After a good lunch we moved to the echoing chapter house, where we interviewed Mr Aziz, who had written something on Henry James. We peppered him with questions, which he answered with ease and good sense, and we agreed that he had passed with flying colours.

In early September I met Edith Evans at Darlington, and talked to her all the next morning. She rested for two hours after lunch, and in the evening gave a first-class poetry recital in the Georgian Theatre. Next day we drove her to Crathorne for lunch. On the way June said: 'I always feel nervous going to grand places and meeting new people.' Edith said: 'NERVOUS?' in her Lady Bracknell voice. 'I just tell myself I'm *adorable.*'

On 13 September I took Bishop Moorman and his wife to see Marrick Priory and they came home to tea.

Mumsy was staying with us. One day we drove her to Saltburn and had sandwiches and tea in sun on the beach. Soon after that we took her to see a play called *Five Finger Exercise* in the Georgian Theatre. It was all about a family accusing each other of sexual malpractice. Mumsy watched enthralled and as we left the theatre she said: 'I always like a nice family play.' The darling old creature insisted on washing all the bedroom curtains, several of which came to pieces in her hands. She also sewed lavender bags from our shredded lavender. We took her to see *Doctor Zhivago* in the Richmond cinema, which has now ceased to exist.

Every time we went to Hawes to shop we talked to Kit Calvert, who collected books about Yorkshire. As he often had to buy a bundle to get a single book, he filled a tiny shop with all the books in the bundles that he didn't want. They were priced at sixpence and a shilling and I got some fine bargains there.

At the beginning of October, Joyce, Reggie and Hugh Wheeler came up for three nights, on two of which Joyce gave performances of her sketches in the Georgian Theatre to packed houses. Then I went up to London for two nights, for the London Library and Literary Society, and stayed happily with Danny and John in Dean's Yard.

On 17 October, at the invitation of Douglas Grant, I made a twenty-minute speech from the top of the stairs of the Leeds Library, to celebrate its centenary for the large crowd below. The following day William Plomer came to stay, and we took him to a concert in the Georgian Theatre, in which Yehudi Menuhin and his sister gave a lovely recital.

On 25 October Micheál Mac Liammóir paid his second visit and at the Georgian Theatre performed *Talking with my Friends*. One morning when June was working at the kitchen sink Micheál came into the room and behind her back he said: 'You beautiful creature, no wonder so many come to see you.' June said: 'What rubbish you do talk, Micheál.' He said: 'No, darling, I wasn't talking to you. I was talking to myself in the mirror.'

Early in November, I was suddenly called on to make speeches. For some unknown reason I made one as guest of honour at the annual dinner of the Darlington branch of the British Medical Association. I kept them amused with some childish stories: '*Question*. What would you give an elephant with diarrhoea? *Answer*. Plenty of room.' A few days later I spoke on publishing to the Richmond Rotary lunch at the King's Head.

Mumsy came for Christmas, and as I wrote in my diary: 'She cleaned and tidied the whole house.' On 31 December I wrote: 'So ends a very happy year, thanks entirely to my darling June.'

[6]

21 January 1969. Deirdre came for a fortnight. I spent several days rearranging all the books at Aske Hall. We took D. to see the Bowes Museum. All this time I was working hard at the Max

Arran beach

catalogue and June typed the pages as I went along. And all the time we were gradually typing and arranging my correspondence with George Lyttelton.

6 April.   Easter. Four Russells – Brian, Vidge and their children Fran and Jonty – arrived in a caravan. Boyk took Jonty fishing and he caught three trout in the beck.

17 April.   Mumsy came to stay and washed everything.

18 April.   Nancy Crathorne died. Lunch at Mulgrave Castle. Bought Valentine table at Pickering for £3 10s. Read lesson at Nancy's funeral.

12 June.   To Garden House at Gatehouse of Fleet. Our first wedding anniversary. Gave June presents in bed. Reached Lagg Hotel on Arran at 8.30 p.m. The island looking lovelier than ever. During our happy fortnight there we explored every part of the island, coastwise and inland, seeing every sort of land and sea birds, and very sad to leave this beloved island. Got home to find seventy letters waiting to be answered.

23 June.   The Queen Mother visited the Georgian Theatre to see a performance of Wycherley's *Country Wife*. I made a speech from the stage, welcoming Her Majesty and paying a loving tribute to the memory of Nancy Crathorne, who had resurrected the theatre. Champagne and conversation with QM in the interval, she as charming as ever.

30 July.   Drove to Scarborough in lovely weather. Great difficulty parking car, a massive crowd waiting to get into cricket ground, gave that up and lunched happily on the beach and lay in the sun. Home by 6 p.m.

In early August we drove round and visited the family, Duff, Bridget, Deirdre, June's family and Mumsy.

Then came our second and much more successful visit to Scarborough. We took a huge bedroom and bathroom in the Grand Hotel, overlooking the sea. On the first day of the cricket match Graeme Pollock of South Africa scored 101 in fifty-two minutes. There were two more enjoyable days of sun and cricket before we drove home.

Mowing with Boyk

At home, I was doing most of the mowing while Boyk built up the stone walls. When that job was finished I gladly handed over the lawn-mower to him.

The last months of 1969 were busy. In September Ernest Mehew and his wife Joy came to stay. When I first knew Ernest he was a civil servant and I used to tease him for being in charge of the department of damaged cheese. He had helped me enormously with the Oscar Wilde letters and other books. Now we discussed Robert Louis Stevenson, on whom Ernest became the greatest living authority. He worked for twenty years collecting all Stevenson's letters, and in 1994 he published them in eight volumes. In 1997 he received a D.Litt. from Edinburgh University.

I was now working hard on Max's catalogue and his *Last Theatres*. My friend Nico Llewelyn-Davies told us of a firm that hired out jigsaw puzzles. We joined it and have enjoyed that peaceful occupation ever since.

Boyk on his birthday with Joyce and June

On 5 October we celebrated Boyk's fifty-seventh birthday. Later that month I resigned from the chairmanship of the London Library, which I had held for twelve years, and was made Vice-President and honorary life member.

Three days later I was offered £20,000 to write the life of Somerset Maugham, but I knew enough of his life to refuse this princely offer.

[7]

Early in 1970, having been told by a local expert that, owing to our geographical position, we should never be able to get a good TV picture, we boldly ordered a set, which with one aerial could get only BBC2, so we sent the whole contraption back. Very soon we discovered that, with two aerials and a booster, we could get excellent pictures.

With Mumsy

Now I must mention my lifelong liking for the works of E. Phillips Oppenheim, rightly known as the Prince of Story-tellers. I started to collect his books when I was at school and continued steadily until I had amassed ninety volumes. Then came a moment in my early grown-up period when I thought this was a childish habit, and I gave all my volumes to a hospital library. Gradually the habit returned, and when I learnt that Nico Llewelyn-Davies had the best collection in the world I sent him the only two volumes I had that were autographed by the author, and in return he sent me a dozen other first editions of which he had duplicates. Now dear Nico is dead, and I don't know what happened to his collection, but by 1970 I had a hundred and fifty volumes, which I believe is almost a complete set. In my old age I read them happily one after another, for they always have a good plot and one never knows what's going to happen next.

Mumsy's seventy-third birthday was on 27 April, and she found ten cards and eleven presents on the breakfast table.

On 30 May the refurbished Marrick Priory was officially opened by the Marquis of Normanby, the Lord Lieutenant of the North Riding, and the building and its chapel were rededicated by the Bishop of Ripon. The Brass Band of the neighbouring village of Reeth begged to be allowed to take part in the service, because they said many of their ancestors were buried in Marrick churchyard. The little chapel was at one end of the building, and at the other end, with several rooms intervening, was the tall clock-tower. We put the band into the foot of the tower, and they played the first two verses of the hymn. Then the Bishop donned his tall headdress and took up his official rod, and just before he started to speak the band struck up another verse of the hymn. We couldn't see or stop them, and I got the giggles, which I was able to hide behind a pillar in the chapel. June was biting her lips to prevent laughter. After a short time the band realised that no one was singing and so fell silent, and the dedication proceeded smoothly.

A day or two later I received a letter from Lord Normanby, saying how well we had done so far, and clearly all we needed was a bungalow for the warden to live in. He enclosed a cheque for £5,000. Until the bungalow was built the warden and his wife lived in a nearby village, where we had rented a house for them.

We were miraculously lucky with our first warden, the Revd Jonathan Bailey, who had every good quality we could have prayed for. He built the foundation of the success which the Young People's Adventure Centre has enjoyed to this day.

On 12 June we happily drove to Arran via Gatehouse of Fleet and a new ship the *Caledonia*, to be comfortably installed in the Lagg Hotel. The good Mr Crook, who ran the hotel, once ran into June on the stairs, couldn't remember her name and said 'Good morning, Lady Um', which I often called her thereafter. Our bedroom and bathroom were first-rate, and so was the food.

The weather was hot and sunny. One day we watched baby seals basking on rocks in the sea near Lochranza. We always had our lunch and tea in some beautiful place, usually by the sea. But it was very sad to see Cooper Angus Lodge being demolished.

With Deirdre

Emlyn Williams and his two assistants came on 19 July to stay for three nights, on the second of which Emlyn gave an excellent performance in the Georgian Theatre.

Next day Duff telephoned to say that Comfort had died in the night. A blessed relief for her and the children, but many sad and happy memories welled up.

Deirdre, Joyce and Reggie came to stay, bringing presents for June's birthday.

On 15 October I drove to Suffolk to see the Blundens. I wrote in my diary: 'Edmund sweet and pathetic. Claire wonderful.'

I picked a lot of apples with Boyk in the orchard, and he said: 'They're mostly nobbut crabs.'

[8]

January 1971 began with snow and a postal strike which lasted for seven weeks, but somehow *The Times* got through to Richmond, whence we had to fetch it.

My ten years' work on the *Catalogue of Max Beerbohm's Caricatures* came to an end in January, when I wrote a long introduction, which June typed, as she had done for the whole book, and it went off in April to Macmillan, who published it on Max's hundredth birthday, 24 August 1972.

Part of the bottom wall of the Marrick churchyard had collapsed, so we took Boyk down to repair it. Stone walls in these parts consist of two outside piles of stone, with rubble in between. Instead of rubble June and I collected all the rubbish that had been thrown away in the churchyard for centuries – broken glass and china, tins and bottles, and we gathered enough to fill Boyk's hollow. When he had finished he said: 'Next time this wall falls down someone will get a surprise.'

My teeth had been gradually deteriorating, and I had already had five removed. Now at 11.15 on 4 June I had two more removed with an anaesthetic, but the dentist must have punctured some vein from which he couldn't stop the blood flowing. He patched it up as best he could and sent me home, where I watched the Test Match on television. But the bleeding continued and Boyk and June drove me back to the dentist, who, after a vain two-hour struggle, sent me in an ambulance to the Military Hospital at Catterick. I was greeted by the duty officer. I asked him if he was a dentist and he replied:

'No, I'm a gynaecologist.' A lieutenant-colonel dentist was soon found, who, with three other dentists and two doctors, worked on me till 9.30 p.m. They tried everything they could think of to stop the bleeding and eventually stitched over the cavity with a plastic splint. When they had finished I was too weak to stand up, so I was wheeled into the intensive care ward. There was only one other patient there, an elderly man with a snore like a foghorn. I was given a saline glucose drip in my arm. There was one nurse in the ward and a young male orderly. He came over to me and said: 'Excuse me, sir, but your shirt is covered with blood. Would you like me to wash and iron it ready for the morning?' 'Yes please', I said, and he did a splendid job on the shirt. The bleeding stopped at midnight, after which I was able to sleep. In the morning Boyk and June drove me home, and after watching some of the Test Match I went to bed for the rest of the day. Two days later my dentist removed splint and stitches, but my mouth was painful for several days.

On 11 June we drove through fog and rain to the Garden House at Gatehouse of Fleet, and next day happily on to the Lagg Hotel.

Two days later was our third wedding anniversary, and I had secretly bought and smuggled across in the car a Brexton picnic set, consisting of a kettle, gas-burner, four cups, saucers and plates. It has been a boon to us and is still available after twenty-five years. We usually ate our lunch and tea in some lovely place or, if it was raining, in the car. Even more than before we enjoyed watching a great many mergansers, gannets and other sea-birds. The only sad thing we saw was the pile of rubble which had been Cooper Angus Lodge.

One day, immediately after we had parked our car near Lochranza, a water-wagtail alighted on the bonnet and attacked its image in the driving mirror. When we came back two-and-a-half hours later, it was still on the attack!

After a happy fortnight we left Arran sunburnt and glowing. We went by ferry to Tarbert and then drove up the west coast of Scotland, through Ardpatrick, Oban, Fort William and Plockton, to which we took a great fancy. Then to Kyle of Lochalsh, where we stayed and had a good dinner at an expensive hotel. Next morning we crossed by five-minute ferry to Skye, where we spent the rest of the day.

Next day we drove through the outskirts of Inverness and Nairn, on southwards, and just before we reached the hotel at Braemar after driving for 174 miles, we saw a red squirrel on the banks of the Dee. Next day on to Blairgowrie and Perth, Dumfriesshire and the Forth bridge, drove through sweltering Edinburgh to Melrose, where we stayed the night.

In the morning we explored Melrose Abbey, then drove for home, via Jedburgh and Carter Bar. At 3 p.m. the clutch of the car collapsed a mile north of Tow Law. We freewheeled to a garage, from which we telephoned to our car-expert in Darlington, and while he was coming to tow us back, we watched the men's final at Wimbledon on the garage's television set. At Darlington we had to transfer all the messy contents of our car into another, in which he drove us home. We were delighted to see Boyk and Nell, but less delighted to find sixty-eight letters waiting to be answered.

My memory of these past years is helped by June's memory and my daily diary. For some forgotten reason the pages between 4 June and 13 September 1971 are blank, and all I can say is that, except for four days watching cricket at Scarborough, we were at home all the time, during which twenty-five of our dearest friends and relations came to stay, apart from those who came for lunch or supper.

On 15 June we spent all day driving 308 miles to stay with Mumsy in her bungalow at Walkford. On the next two days we visited June's sister Betty and other relations, then returned home through a mass of summer traffic.

One sunny day an old army friend dropped in on his way south with a colleague of his in the paint business. We took them round the house and garden and then settled them on the terrace to enjoy the sunshine and the view. Suddenly the colleague said to me: 'You know, if you're living in this beautiful place and doing the things you want

June, Boyk and Joyce

to do, you're halfway to Heaven.' I don't, alas, remember his name or his appearance, but 'his words wing on as live words will'.[1]

Early in July Joyce and Reggie came to stay and on the afternoon of Saturday 10 July they were sitting with us on our terrace in blazing hot sun. Suddenly Boyk appeared. Joyce and Reggie already knew Boyk well and we all talked happily away. We pointed out to Boyk that on the wall of the house a fly-catcher was making its little nest inside a deserted blackbird's larger one. Boyk said he'd never seen such a thing before and he fetched a ladder so that he could see it at close range.

Eventually Boyk left us and walked up the field between our house and his. About three-quarters of the way up he stopped to have a chat with his farmer friend John Horn, who was harvesting the hay. Suddenly, in the middle of their talk, Boyk keeled over and fell heavily

1 Thomas Hardy on George Meredith.

to the ground. The doctor was sent for, but Boyk was obviously dead, his heart, which had been troubling him for some years, suddenly gave out, and he died in a second without pain or knowledge.

I asked if I might say a few words about Boyk at his funeral, because he was such a very special person:

> Most of you knew him for very much longer than I did, but for the past six years I have seen him every day, often for several hours at a stretch, and the better I got to know him the more did I admire, respect and love him.
>
> In the course of a fairly long and busy life I have known some thousands of men, young and old, rich and poor, town and country, and I can truthfully say that I never met a more remarkable or a more lovable man than Boyk.
>
> He never came to church, but in his daily life he was one of the most truly Christian people I have ever known – always ready to help a neighbour in distress. For many years now, in Marske and the surrounding farms, whenever a crisis occurred, the word went out Send for Boyk, and Boyk always came and fettled things up. Once he knew and liked you there was absolutely *nothing* he wouldn't do for you.
>
> Jesus said It is more blessed to give than to receive, and Boyk loved giving, just as he often didn't much like receiving, since his pride and independence made him dislike feeling under an obligation.
>
> You would have expected him to know all about the farming in which he had been brought up – all about lambing and haytime and the care of beasts and all the rest. It says in the Bible 'Some there be that have no memorial', but Boyk has his memorial in the lovely dry-stone walls he built at the bottom of the new churchyard and below, and the two he recently put up at Marrick Priory. When he first began to lay some flagged paths for me, and had done about five yards perfectly, I said 'I can see you've done this before, Boyk.' To which he answered: 'I've never laid a flagged path before in my life.' Yet he knew instinctively how it should be done, how

you shouldn't lay two long stones together, how to get the right balance and trim. In this, as in everything else, he was a perfectionist, satisfied only with the best he could do, and I have often seen him heave out a huge flag when the cement was almost dry, or take down a section of wall he had just built, because he knew he could do it better. He was an artist with a spade or any other tool – quick and neat and sure.

In the same way he had an instinctive knowledge of machines, and could quickly understand the working of a new one he had never seen before.

When he took up gardening, which was undoubtedly the great passion of his last years, he rapidly became expert and creative, though seeds and plants never grew quickly enough to satisfy his impatient desire for perfection. 'You must plant everything with love', he used to say with a broad smile, 'and then it will grow.'

He was a man of outstanding intelligence and vivid imagination, of scrupulous integrity and complete loyalty, of unfailing sympathy and warmth. His sense of humour was superb. He loved pulling people's legs, and having his own pulled in return. He had a rich and instantaneous flow of wit and repartee, a great gift for saying the unexpected thing, and all our hours together were filled with jokes and laughter.

He was interested in everything and everybody. To all our guests, from children to eighty-year-olds, he talked with equal ease, and they all loved him.

He died as he would have wished to die, standing in the field between his house and ours, talking to an old friend, in a split second. He was such an active outdoor man that the life of an invalid was unthinkable for him.

He was particularly blessed in his marriage. He and Nellie were perfect complements to each other, and her dry sense of humour wonderfully balanced Boyk's exuberant flights of fancy. To be with them in their house, as we often were, and to join in their loving banter, was a perpetual delight. It is to Nellie now, in her shock and grief, that all our hearts are turned.

I am sure that I am speaking the thoughts of everyone here when I say that for the rest of our lives my wife and I will cherish the memory of Boyk – always with sorrow at the loss of our nearest and dearest friend, but above all with joy and laughter, with gratitude and love.

On 27 August Adam's son Jason was born.

In October the cellist Paul Tortelier gave a superb performance in the Georgian Theatre, accompanied by two members of his family playing other instruments. By this time I was chairman of the Georgian Theatre Trust, and also chairman of the Marrick Priory committee, both of which bodies held monthly meetings.

[9]

At the beginning of 1972 I was working on a volume of Max Beerbohm's uncollected pieces of prose, which was published later that year as *A Peep into the Past and Other Prose Pieces*.

The University of York very kindly allowed us to use their microfilm to search in *The Times* for some detail of a Max Beerbohm caricature. As June was working the microfilm machine I suddenly said 'Stop', for I had noticed a short unsigned article about William Archer, which I was sure must have been written by Max. We wrote to *The Times* and they confirmed that it was indeed by Max. A splendid piece of serendipity which I included in *A Peep into the Past*.

In those days sales of village furniture and so on were carried out in the garden and sometimes in the road. In the middle of January we went to a village sale at Redmire and bought a mass of china, five chairs, a mirror and two fenders for £19. Nowadays, alas, all such bargains are rushed to a central saleroom in the nearest town.

There were constant power-failures that winter, but we sat cosily by the fireside in the little sitting-room; and June cooked on the calor-gas burner.

In March we visited a village sale at Horsehouse, and bought a hoover, an electric fire, many pots, pans, glasses, mugs and plates for

£15; and at a later sale in Richmond covered market we bought, mostly for the cottage, a wardrobe (50p), a chest of drawers (£1), a single bed, three electric fires (£4), two rugs, two fenders, an ironing board, a watering can and sundry plates. All hands, Nell and Willie Longstaff, a retired farmer who had taken over Boyk's gardening, stone-walling and odd jobs, worked hard on the cottage.

At Easter-time the Russells and their children came for a long weekend. On one day we walked them up to Summer Lodge Tarn, a high-up and very beautiful lake, on three sides of which hundreds of seagulls nest every year. If one goes too near they fly screeching away, but if one watches one can see that each returning bird immediately recognises its own nest.

On 9 June, on the way to our beloved Arran, we drove up to spend the night with K. Elliott at Harwood on the Scottish borders. She was a remarkable woman, the fifteenth child of Sir Charles Tennant Bart and elder sister of Nancy Crathorne. She married Colonel Walter Elliot, and after his death was awarded a seat in the House of Lords as Baroness Elliot of Harwood, and she regularly commuted from the Scottish Lowlands to the House of Lords. But to all her friends she was just dear K.

The Lagg Hotel was as welcoming and as efficient as ever. Wherever we were we listened to a Test Match on our portable radio. A gloriously hot and sunny day for our fourth wedding anniversary. At Whiting Bay I bought June a gay leather bag and she bought me my first anorak.

On our last Arran day we walked up to the headland, just in time to eat a sandwich lunch before heavy rain fell and drenched us as we walked down, but we were gladdened by coming across a herd of some fifty red deer with young ones very close. Another night at Gatehouse of Fleet and on 25 June we were home again with fifty-two letters waiting to be answered.

After four days watching cricket at Scarborough we set off for Elba on 11 September. A very different journey from our easy drive to Arran – one night in London, cross Channel, change trains in Paris, one night on express train to Pisa, then train to Piombino, boat to Elba and a drive across the island on the 13th. It was a lovely day and when we got to L'Etrusca we were greeted by Jane, a good-looking Englishwoman who ran the hotel and lived in a flat with her sister Harriet. The ten bedrooms were a little distance from the main building and above it on a steep little hill. They were accessible by road, but more quickly up a lot of rather rickety steps. We had a comfortable room, with shower and WC attached, and a little terrace outside facing south. On a clear day we could just see the Isle of Monte Cristo.

Whenever it was fine enough we had breakfast, lunch and dinner out of doors. The chef Angelino was a master craftsman, giving us a variety of delicious dishes and a different ice-cream each day. We drank very good red and white Italian wine. On our first full day there the sunny morning turned into torrential rain for the rest of the day. Jane drove up in her car to fetch us to dinner and drove us back afterwards. Most of our days there were hot and sunny, and we spent most of them on an empty beach just along the shore, where we swam, paddled and lay in the sun.

In October we happily returned to our usual home pursuits – writing and answering letters and working in all parts of the garden, with television and jigsaws in evening. From the 16th to the 19th I was in bed with a mysterious illness.

In November there was plenty of snow, but the Normanbys and the Baileys managed to come to lunch together. I started working on the autobiography of Arthur Ransome, who had left it for me to get in order.

For some time I had been subject to dizzy and groggy periods. Dr Saunders of Middlesborough diagnosed my condition as Menière's disease of which I was gradually cured.

Mumsy came for Christmas and as usual sewed, laundered and mended everything within sight.

[10]

Most of January 1973 was overshadowed by the periodical dizziness of Menière's disease. Drs Heron and Ward came from Richmond to give me injections, and Dr Saunders from Middlesbrough came to change my pills. I never knew when the next bout of giddiness might occur, but we cheered ourselves up by buying a colour television set and peacefully enjoying our jigsaws. By the beginning of February my illness was receding, and I was able to resume my usual happy life, and after some weeks I smoked my first pipe without ill effects.

In April Mumsy came for her seventy-sixth birthday and we gave her thirteen presents. At the end of the month dear Arthur Cave suddenly died. He was the nicest, kindest and wisest vicar I've ever known. We sadly attended his funeral.

Duff had begun to write his life of Peter Fleming and sent us each chapter as he finished it. We sent them back with a few minor criticisms and much praise.

In May we spent two days in Deirdre's new house in Lewes, arranging her books. On 21 May Harry Fairhurst, the librarian of York University, came to lunch with his chief cataloguer Lois Gordon. They said they would like to catalogue our library, and we arranged for Lois to start on 1 October.

In June we spent two nights with K. Elliot at Harwood and then happily drove to Ardrossan to embark for Arran. Delighted to be in the Lagg Hotel again. Our fortnight there was as carefree and happy as it had been the year before.

The next two months were homely and peaceful. I helped Brownlee Kirkpatrick with the bibliography of Edmund Blunden, but the commonest entry in my diary was 'Read in the library'.

Phylla came with her children Guy and Alice, and we took them to the beach at Saltburn, and at night the two little ones slept in tiny tents on the front lawn. And all the time Willie was gradually building an excellent stone wall at the top of the back lawn.

Junie and I were both vaccinated against cholera, which was then rampant in Italy.

On 11 September we went to London by train and put our luggage in Bridget's flat in Vicarage Gate. In the afternoon we had a lively tea in Tommy Lascelles's residence in the grounds of Kensington Palace, then walked down to 79 Victoria Road,

Boyk, June, Nanny, Phylla, Duff, Guy and Alice

Kensington, where the occupants very kindly let us see the tiny bedroom in which I was born. That evening we went to a thriller play *Sleuth*, which we both thoroughly enjoyed; and then back to Vicarage Gate for the night.

Next day we began the journey to Elba again, with a night in the train, and we were given a warm welcome by Jane, Harriet and Angelino. As we ate our usual delicious dinner one of the waiters said there would be a sirocco the following day. And he was right. A strong south wind all day and no sun. Read on our bed and walked down to our favourite beach. Thereafter the weather improved and I swam twice each day. And so our happy holiday continued.

One day Vernon Bartlett and his wife drove over for lunch and left their dog shut in their car. All through lunch Mrs B kept worrying about the dog. 'Now he's in the front seat', to which Vernon said: 'Don't worry, dear, he hasn't got the ignition key.'

Soon we were the only guests left in the hotel and Jane insisted on our moving down to the luxury flat. Left sadly on 27 September. Our bill seemed reasonable at 176,000 lire. On board the ship we bought tax-free malt whisky, cigarettes, tobacco and scent. Stayed the night at Vicarage Gate, and the next day returned home.

In my non-stop working years in London 1946–64 I often longed for peace and quiet. It's true that I had restful times at Kisdon, but what I longed for was 'a house full of books and a garden of flowers'[1], so my dream had turned to reality.

In the autumn we were happily rustic. On 3 October Harry Fairhurst brought Lois Gordon over from York and we settled her in the cottage, where she stayed for six months. She catalogued fifty-nine books in her first morning.

On 7 October I read the lesson at the harvest festival service, and Ernest Mehew and I astonished June and Joy by lustily singing 'We plough the fields and scatter the good seed on the land.'

While we were on holiday in Elba my dear friend William Plomer had died and left me as his literary executor. So we now drove down to Hassocks in Sussex, where he had lived, and piled the car high with all his letters, papers and books. When we got them home we spent a lot of time sorting them and then gave them to Durham University, where they were well received. On five days a week Lois had lunch and tea with us, and we drove her to Richmond to shop. I worked on preparing William's autobiography for the printer.

On 7 November we went up to London to attend William's memorial service at St Martin-in-the-Fields. There was a large congregation and many of his literary and musical friends took part in the service. I'm sure he would have approved of everything.

For Christmas we entertained Mumsy, Deirdre and her daughters Susie and Lucy.

1 Andrew Lang, *Ballade of True Wisdom.*

[11]

I spent most of January and February 1974 working on Arthur Ransome's autobiography. He wrote most of it between the ages of sixty-five and seventy-seven and he several times made me promise that, if necessary, I would edit and see it through the press. This would have presented few difficulties had it not been for the unusual way he wrote his books. With *Swallows and Amazons* and its eleven successors it was his habit to prepare an extremely detailed synopsis, complete with chapter-titles, so that he knew exactly what was to happen in each chapter. He would then begin writing whichever chapter took his fancy or seemed easiest, leaving the most difficult to the last. Thus a surviving page of his work-sheet for *Pigeon Post* shows that at one point he had written and revised nineteen of the first twenty-nine chapters, leaving Chapters 2, 4, 7, 10, 11, 13, 18, 19, 23 and 25 still to be written. Reading the smooth-flowing narrative, building up to a climax, it is difficult to believe that the book was written in this extraordinary way, but so it was.

When it came to his autobiography, written over more than a decade of his old age, this idiosyncratic mode of composition left many problems for his editor. Characters introduced in later chapters were often introduced again and again in earlier chapters, written years later. A great deal of repetition had to be removed, and passages transposed, so that people were introduced on their first appearance. I had to spend a lot of time on the book, which was published by Cape in 1976.

I sadly heard from Claire Blunden that Edmund died on 21 January. Four days later we drove to Long Melford for the funeral, at which an old ex-army comrade laid a wreath of Flanders poppies on the grave.

Duff came with the complete typescript of his life of Peter Fleming, and we went carefully through it together.

I read the lessons in church every Sunday, and there were seldom more than a dozen worshippers.

Sonnet from Edmund
Blunden in my
Jonathan Cape days

On 7 March I gave the address at Edmund Blunden's memorial service at St Bride's in Fleet Street. Towards the end of March Lois finished her cataloguing and Harry Fairhurst fetched her four days later.

I wrote an article on Siegfried for the *Dictionary of National Biography*. Then I started reading his diaries, of which I eventually published three volumes.

Mumsy came for her seventy-eighth birthday, and we once again gave her thirteen presents.

On 9 August, Junie's fiftieth birthday, I surprised her by having a Mini delivered for her. She was stupefied when she saw it.

At the end of that month I began to have stomach pains, cause unknown, so we reluctantly decided we ought to cancel our visit to

Elba. To cheer me on my sixty-seventh birthday Junie gave me a
bright red shirt, a bottle of malt whisky, two gramophone records, an
electric mosquito-repellent and some new secateurs. Nell, bless her,
gave me six red handkerchiefs and a box of Thornton's chocolates.

On 2 September I began writing the life of my mother, which
turned into *The Arms of Time*. Next day we visited a specialist in
Darlington, who was reassuring about my stomach pains. So we spent
the weekend at the Beach Hotel at Sandsend, north of Whitby. On
Sunday we drove to Robin Hood's Bay, to which we took a great
fancy.

Early in November two dear friends died on successive days,
Danny's husband John Carleton on the 6th and Eric Linklater on the
7th. John was the nicest of men, and Eric was an old and much loved
friend. He had been wonderfully helpful to me when I started my
publishing business. In 1963 he dedicated to me his novel *A Man Over
Forty* and in my copy he inscribed:

> 'To Rupert Hart-Davis with old affection'
> Originally, my dear Rupert, my dedication was intended as a
> simple gesture of simple friendship. But a day or two ago I
> was re-reading some pages in your majestic array of Oscar
> Wilde's letters, and it struck me that it should, instead, be
> regarded as the stiff salute of an ancient mercenary, still in
> the ranks, to a new and brilliant Company Commander. Well,
> take it either way. Affection and respect are both sincere. ERIC

On 14 November there was a dedication service at Marrick Priory.
I read the lesson. Over 150 people were there.

On Friday 6 December we attended John Carleton's memorial
service in Westminster Abbey – it was superb, especially the trumpets.

On 13 December we filled the car again with William Plomer's
letters, papers and books, and drove to Durham, where they gave us
lunch at the University Club.

A very happy Christmas with Mumsy here. Gave Junie her first
electric typewriter. So ended a very busy and happy year.

[12]

The first months of 1975 were peaceful and I finally finished my edition of Arthur Ransome's autobiography, to which I added a prologue and an epilogue.

In March I had my last eleven teeth removed and my mouth was very painful for days. I hated my false teeth from the beginning and in my eighties I put them away.

Then days later I thankfully resigned from the chairmanship of the Georgian Theatre Trust, though I remained a member of the committee. And then we learned that Arthur Ransome's widow Genia had died, and in due course we had a hideous drive to the Lake District for her funeral. It was an appalling day, a blizzard of snow, hail and sleet. We several times missed our way, arrived late for the funeral service and then stood in pouring rain while she was buried beside Arthur. The village was called Rusland, only one letter short of Russland, the German for Russia, where Arthur met Genia when she was Trotsky's secretary. We again lost our way on the return journey. A horrible day. After Genia's death John Bell and I became Arthur's joint literary executors and equal sharers with the Royal Literary Fund in his royalties, which are still very profitable. Arthur would be delighted by that and by the flourishing Ransome Society.

April and May were peaceful, and on 2 June we set out once more for Elba, first spending a night in London at Bridget's flat after going to tea with Tommy Lascelles, who regaled us with amusing anecdotes of the four monarchs to whom he had been private secretary. In the evening we thoroughly enjoyed *A Little Night Music*, of which our friend Hugh Wheeler wrote the libretto. In the interval we had drinks with Rosamond Lehmann and her grandson. We spent a night in the train from Paris to Pisa, and arrived at L'Etrusca at 5.30 p.m., to find our favourite room, No. 10, at the end of the row. First a Campari and then one of Angelino's most delicious dinners. Although it was two years since our last visit, we felt we had never been away.

The weather was perfect and we swam and sunned and sat on the little terrace beside our room, where I wrote a good deal of *The Arms of Time*, which was not published until 1979. I suddenly became stone-deaf in one ear and could only just hear in the other. We had a happy evening with the girls and the Bartletts, but I caught little of the merry conversation.

Our seventh wedding anniversary was on 13 June. Junie gave me a tobacco-pouch, and I gave her a paperback, a tea-towel and a necklace, and we split two bottles of champagne with the girls and the Bartletts. Still deaf as a haddock. Johnson's Baby Oil brought back some hearing in my left ear, but my right one never recovered. Wonderful food and mostly wonderful weather. Very sad to leave on 18 June.

We found the Old Rectory in perfect condition, having been looked after by Nell and Willie in our absence, and the weather was equal to Elba's. We watched a good deal of Wimbledon and were delighted when Ashe won the men's singles. One day we drove to Barbon Manor in Westmorland and had lunch with Roger and Sibell Fulford.

June in the rockery

And soon afterwards we drove to Kirkdale Farm to lunch with Pinkie and Martyn Beckett, both of us believing ourselves to be half-brothers.

At the end of August Bridget and David brought their children Amy and Simon to stay, and we drove them to Saltburn, where we spent all day on the beach, the children good and happy.

On 3 September we drove to Ardrossan (185 miles) and found ourselves again in our same room in the Lagg Hotel. As usual we were fascinated by the gannets and other sea birds, as well as seals with their young. The Volvo was a godsend, as we were very comfortable in it whenever it rained, which was quite often. After a happy fortnight in changeable weather we drove home through wind and rain.

In November the Baileys came to announce their departure from Marrick Priory – a great blow. Jonathan was to be Vicar of Wetherby. They asked for a recommendation and I sent one saying he was a wonderful man, and ending: 'If he doesn't get to the top there will be something wrong in the Church of England.' He is now, I'm happy to say, a bishop. Needless to say, we had a terrible job to find a new warden to follow Jonathan, but after some early mistakes we found suitable men.

The last two months of 1975 seemed to be non-stop entertaining. In all fifty-six people, friends, relations, strangers, stayed in the house for a night or weekend and a great many came just for a meal. On Christmas Eve there were nine for lunch. Junie produced delicious food for all those hungry mouths.

[13]

On the night of 3 January 1976 the giant chestnut tree in the top edge of our bottom field was blown down over our lawn, where it lay huge and pathetic, its branches almost as high as the house. We were both very sad at this unexpected loss. Also two huge fir-branches were blown down from the churchyard on to our rose-garden. An employee of the church cut up and removed them. Willie began to saw branches off the chestnut, helped by Allan Fawcett, who split and stored logs.

Junie and I began to sort my and George Lyttelton's letters, hoping they might some day appear in print. Allan pulled the trunk of the chestnut over into the field with ropes and tractor, and then cut it up. Luckily the weather in the next few weeks made it impossible for visitors to get here, but in April they began to arrive with the daffodils. On 13 April Jonathan and Susan Bailey came to a farewell dinner before their departure. We gave them a well-known picture of Marrick, and we talked till 11.45 p.m: a very jolly evening.

On 31 May we set off for our annual visit to Elba. We had tea with Tommy Lascelles in his garden, stayed with Danny for the night and then, after the usual journey, we received a rapturous welcome from the girls and a superb dinner from Angelino. We bathed and sunned on all the sunny days and on bad days read our books on the tiny terrace which was protected from the south wind by a mimosa tree, and I finished part one of *The Arms of Time*. Our three weeks passed all too quickly and we sadly kissed the girls goodbye.

The wonderful weather continued right into August. On my sixty-ninth birthday I had a pile of presents, the nicest a wonderfully comfortable outdoor chair, which is still delighting me after twenty years. Junie also gave me several other welcome things, including a bottle of Glenmorangie malt whisky.

On 1 September we happily returned to Arran and the Lagg Hotel, where we had made friends with the new proprietor Mr Hamilton. We were delighted to find that there were more than fourteen brands of malt whisky in the bar, so we could try a different one on every day of our holiday! We drove round the coast to all our favourite places, with lunch and tea in the car. I photographed June 'willing the Brexton to boil'. The weather deteriorated and we decided to go home after ten days. Mr Hamilton was very kind and refused to charge us for the extra five nights.

There was a peaceful interlude at home, and then on 17 October, an ever-remembered day: Jock and Diana Murray came to lunch. Jock and I had been friends since we were at Eton together. There

Jock was John Grey, but his mother was a Murray, and when Sir John Murray, the head of the publishing firm, died, Jock took over and added Murray to his name. During lunch one of them asked me what I was working on. I told them of *The Arms of Time*, which was promised to Jamie Hamilton, and went on to say that June and I were busily putting together my six-year correspondence with George Lyttelton, of which the first year's-worth had been typed. Diana asked if they could look at it. I said certainly, and they took it away with them. Diana liked it very much and passed it to Jock, who liked it too. He was an inspirational publisher, always prepared to take a chance.

On 2 November we drove to Wetherby to lunch with the Baileys. I finished editing William Plomer's posthumous book *Electric Delights* and sent it to Cape.

David's father Malcolm Silsoe died on 6 December, and my Bridget became the Lady Silsoe. A lot of snow failed to spoil our happy Christmas with Mumsy helping Junie a great deal.

[14]

On 6 January 1977 I received a cheque for £500 from W.H. Smith and an appointment to judge their book of the year prize. There was a great deal of snow during the month. On 1 February Jock Murray telephoned to say he would publish all the Lyttelton letters. Great excitement.

A procession of visitors in March left us exhausted after so many days of talking and cooking. Amused and rather flattered to hear that the British Museum copy of *The Letters of Oscar Wilde* had been stolen.

On 26 April Mumsy arrived for her eightieth birthday next day. Great fun watching her opening presents.

On 29 May we again set out for Elba. Before spending the night at Vicarage Gate we visited Tommy Lascelles, taking him a bottle of Montrachet, which pleased him. We had tea in his attractively overgrown garden. Tommy, aged ninety, was in excellent form. Next day,

Alice, Guy, Amy, Simon, Damon and Jason

after lunching with Deirdre, we went to see poor Harriet in a nursing home, a harrowing visit.

The following morning we set off on our journey, sleeping pretty well in the Paris to Pisa train and arrived to a great welcome from Jane. On most of the following days I worked on my book. Junie was trying to master *Italian in Three Months without a Master*, but often slipped back to her thriller.

There was some local excitement during this holiday: five men who had escaped from an island prison recently were believed to be still at large on Elba. Road-blocks were in operation. Junie thought she saw and heard armed police outside our bedroom during the night. Vernon and Jo Bartlett arrived next day.

On one of our last days it was too hot to walk down to the beach at 5.30 p.m. so we sat on our terrace in the shade. A bomb was washed ashore below the restaurant, and they had to send to the mainland for someone to deal with it. A lovely last day, and we were sad to leave all the sun and sea.

On my seventieth birthday on 28 August I had a tremendous surprise. Unknown to me Junie had arranged for all my family to arrive on that morning – Deirdre, my three children with their wives and husband, and six grandchildren. I can't imagine how Junie hid from me all the massive and delicious meals she gave us all. She also hid some garden furniture, which the children helped her to unpack. It was a lovely hot sunny day and we stood the six grandchildren on the garden wall in order of age and size. Adam took the photograph and then got us all together on the terrace, set off his camera and dashed over to join us for more photographs. The dear boy brought me a lovely pipe and *seventy* different kinds of tobacco, which I astonishedly unpacked on the terrace. Another surprise from the family was a music centre – radio, cassette and record-player all in one. In the evening Alice played beautifully on her accordion, Adam and his family drove home, which wasn't far away, and the others slept all over the house, two of the children on the drawing-room floor. Who could have asked for a happier birthday?

My seventieth birthday party

Then in September we spent a happy but rather wet week in our
beloved Arran, visiting all our old haunts. One day a man serving in a
Brodick shop told me that there was an albino deer in Glen Sannox,
and that the last one seen had presaged the death of the Duke.

The rubble of Cooper Angus Lodge had been removed while the
space previously occupied by it and the garden was now a posh
caravan park, with some of the old trees and shrubs preserved.

[15]

For some forgotten reason I kept no diary for 1978 or 1979, but our
visitors' book shows that we had fifty-two staying visitors in 1978 and
thirty-eight in 1979 and for our last visit to Elba in 1978 I kept a little
diary there. On 29 May Danny met us at Paddington and drove us to
Tommy Lascelles. He was now ninety-one but right on the spot, full
of anecdotes and jokes.

Deirdre and her husband William on her birthday

The next day we spent in London. We lunched with Diana Cooper, visited Harriet and were impressed by her improvement since the previous year. We dined and slept at Danny's. Kate Grimond, Peter and Celia Fleming's daughter, was at dinner and I told her a lot about her parents.

Next day we set off for Elba, and a long wait at Pisa enabled us to enjoy the Leaning Tower, which reminded me of the old joke: 'What did the Leaning Tower of Pisa say to Big Ben?' Answer: 'I've got the inclination if you've got the time.' When we arrived there was a warm welcome from Jane and the usual delicious dinner. Next day sun and swimming and, as usual, our siesta after lunch covered two hours.

Next day, 5 June, was the publication day of *Lyttelton* Vol. I and Jane stood us a drink in celebration. Inspired by that I dragged *The Arms of Time* on to 1923, only four years from its finish. And so our regular days continued with sun and delicious meals. Angelino was as ever, a genius at inventing new dishes.

On 12 June a 'wonderfully exciting express letter' arrived from Jock's partner Roger Hudson. A sweating motor-cyclist brought it all the way across Elba. In it was a copy of Philip Ziegler's stunningly good review of *Lyttelton* Vol. I in *The Times*. He described the book as 'the last fine flower of Augustan England', and said of me: 'If he had devoted to making money half the energy he put into works of scholarship and the helping of his friends he would have retired a millionaire.'

Next day was our tenth wedding anniversary, and we gave each other surprise presents which turned out to be identical tiny boxes. I wrote to Philip and to Roger Hudson and worked at my book. We had a very nice letter from Harriet, difficult to read but very affectionate and well expressed.

On 16 June everything went wrong – electricity, coffee machine, etc. It all seemed to suit Jane and I thought that perhaps with so much on her mind she had no time to worry about Harriet and her own health. Anyhow she was an angel of goodness to us.

The following day I finished the first draft of my book, having written 10,000 words since we came to Elba. Our last two days were

Pesky in her early days

all sun and swimming, and we were sad to leave; we had no idea that it was to be our last visit to the island.

Very soon after we got home a new character came into our lives. We were both weeding in the rose-garden when a young man walked past carrying a tiny kitten. He said he had found it wandering on the road and he went round the village asking everyone if it belonged to them. Having drawn a blank he came back rather depressed, and we both realised that we must take the kitten home, which we did after borrowing a tin of cat-food from our tenants in the cottage. The young man was most relieved and grateful.

The first night she crept behind a potato-pot beside the kitchen sink and went to sleep there. Next night she got into the kitchen table drawer from the inside, and if she hadn't jumped out in the morning before we opened the drawer she might have been beheaded. We decided to call her Pesky, an American word meaning tiresome, but despite bits of tiresomeness she entwined herself in our hearts for the next eleven years.

We went cricket-watching at Scarborough at the end of August for four days, and Nell looked after Pesky while we were away. We got a rapturous reception from the little creature when we returned home. Nothing of interest happened during the rest of 1978, and we settled down to a peaceful time with Pesky and Mumsy for Christmas.

[16]

At the beginning of 1979 we sadly agreed that we couldn't go to Elba again, having Pesky to look after, but at the end of August we did spend four days cricket-watching at Scarborough again. In June we had gone up to London for the day, seeing Deirdre and visiting Harriet, then picked up Mumsy and took her home.

During 1979 I had four books published: *The Arms of Time, Lyttelton* Vol. II, *Two Men of Letters* (correspondence between R.C. Hutchinson and Martyn Skinner) and *Selected Letters of Oscar Wilde*. All of them received favourable notices in the papers. For instance, someone in *British*

With June

Book News said of *Lyttelton*: 'The book belongs in that wide category, embracing Boswell's *Life of Johnson* and Tuckwell's *Reminiscences of Oxford*, that in a hundred different ways informs, challenges and stimulates while recording the everyday life of sharply delineated characters.'

Of *The Arms of Time* Anthony Powell wrote in the *Daily Telegraph*: 'This memoir, sad, funny, moving, intensely felt, could have been written only by Rupert Hart-Davis: partly because the author has a peculiar skill in telling a story which in many hands might have been too inward-looking, even embarrassing. The tact and humour which made his biography of Hugh Walpole (1952) a model of its kind are here used with an even more remarkable delicacy and dexterity.'

Later in the year we thought we had lost Pesky. She disappeared for forty-eight hours. We were sure she must have met with disaster and were very sad, until on the third morning I found her in her basket looking far from well. We rushed her off to the vet, who said she had a broken jaw, which he mended with a strong piece of wire. We were pretty sure she must have been hit by a motor-car, was probably unconscious for a long time, and then, unbelievably, came up across a big field and through the two cat-flaps, into the back kitchen, where she slept in her basket on top of a chest. Very soon she seemed to be out of pain, and when we took her back to have the wire removed, the vet said her jaw was perfectly in place.

[17]

We had a peaceful year in 1980 with no Pesky accidents, but in March I heard that dear Frank Swinnerton's wife had had a stroke. He was ninety-six, and she a few years younger. I telephoned to Danny, who was or had been the head of the Royal Literary Fund, and she promptly wrote to Frank, rang the RLF and told them to send him £1,000.

Theatre and Marrick meetings continued, and I began to think I'd had enough of them. I was busy sorting out and editing Siegfried Sassoon's diaries, which Junie faithfully typed out for me.

We drove down to spend a couple of nights with Mumsy, and at the end of August spent our usual four days at Scarborough.

[18]

The new year, 1981, started with a tragedy. Junie's brother John rang to say that Mumsy was very ill. Junie rushed down to Walkford on 28 February, and on that day Mumsy was taken to hospital. On 5 March she underwent an operation, and next day she was unconscious, but on the day after that Junie and John were amazed at how good and cheerful she was. Next day she was distressed and wandering, and on 9 March she died. The funeral was on 12 March and Junie got home two days later.

I wrote her a letter every day she was away, mostly love-letters, but also to let her know all details of life at the Old Rectory, and most of the following paragraphs are quotations from my letters. Danny left to go to Edinburgh, and Pesky was a great comfort. Nell came down every day. I sat up till all hours waiting for a call from Junie, only to discover that all the telephones in the village were out of order. Pesky was clinging pretty close to me. There was plenty for me to eat in the house, but it seemed terribly empty and silent. I was still at work on *Lyttelton* IV.

I was so touched by all your little things about the house, and from time to time I felt rather weepy. 'Don't whimper, poor old sod', I say to myself. 'You'll soon be with your Junie again.'

One day Pesky brought a live baby rabbit into the house, but Nell was clever enough to liberate it. Pesky slept on me from 2.30 to 4, and then had a good purring scrabble under the lapels of my jacket. I know she misses you and is putting up with me. I must confess that after you rang off this morning I had a little cry for darling old Mumsy. She was so dear and affectionate and brave and funny, and I truly loved her.

I can quite understand why people living alone are apt to go round the house groaning, whimpering and talking to themselves, as Siegfried used to do in his old age. The proofs of his diary are wonderfully free of any but printers' errors – all due to your beautiful re-typing. Nell asked me to meals, but I told her I was hard put to eat all the food here.

On 2 June we drove to Durham University where, after an ample lunch, at which Junie sat next the Vice-Chancellor, I, with a number of other men, was awarded a D.Litt. The professor who read out the commendation got it all wrong, saying that I was being honoured for

Portraits of June and me in 1981 and 1982 by David Hankinson

helping to sort William Plomer's papers, whereas in fact William left all his papers to me, and I had sorted them at home and then given them to Durham, because it was the only university that ever gave him anything.

Later in the month we spent a happy week on Arran with Deirdre and her husband William, and later four days at Scarborough.

If I printed a list of all the friends and relations who in that or any other year came here for a meal, for the day or the weekend, it would look like a mishmash out of *Who's Who*. The following year saw the publication of *Lyttelton* III and the first volume of Siegfried's diaries.

[19]

Looking through our visitors' book for 1982 I see that forty people stayed in the house during the year, and many others came to lunch or tea. Junie managed to give them all delicious food without any help. Pesky was our love and joy.

The fourth Lyttelton volume was published during the year, and much of its success came as a result of the BBC having broadcast several programmes from the previous volumes, in which my cousin John Julius Norwich read my letters.

In September we made our final visit to Scarborough.

[20]

At the end of January 1983 I began to write my diary again. I was correcting the proofs of *A Beggar in Purple*, a selection from my common-place book, which was published by Hamish Hamilton later in the year. A great deal of snow was falling, but the snow-plough got through to the village, refusing to clear the little lane up to the church and our house. Happily the invaluable Mr Binks got his travelling food-shop right up to us. I did some overhauling and tidying of my laden desk (this action is still very necessary in 1998). Worked on *Lyttelton* VI, the last of the series.

After some negotiations with the University of Tulsa, Oklahoma, we sold my library to them for £200,000, of which they sent £25,000 now. The books don't go to them till I'm dead.

I was very touched by my old friend Ray Bradbury sending me a paperback edition of his collected poems.

The *Sunday Telegraph* began serialising Siegfried's *War Diaries 1915–18*, which Faber was to publish later that year. Junie, bless her, finished typing the 318 pages of Siegfried's 1923–25 diaries. We celebrated with a half-bottle of Moët et Chandon.

On 12 March Junie went on an organised walk with Pat Medley. She was away from 1 till 4 p.m., and Pesky spent a lot of the time looking for her. Eventually she lay on the back lawn until Junie drove back in her Mini, and then jumped into the car to welcome her home.

Next day I listened to my radio interview with Frank Delaney, which was much better than I had expected. Junie made a tape of it. My editions of Siegfried's war diaries and his war poems were published, and I received a great many pleasing letters about them.

Diana Hood brought poor old Roger Fulford over, wheelchair and all. His wits were okay, but his speech was difficult, yet he was his old sweet self. It was the last time we saw him.

A hundred copies of *Lyttelton* V and two hundred jiffy-bags arrived by carrier. A lot of inscribing and posting to be done! A nice royalty cheque for £1,500 arrived from Jock Murray. Meanwhile I was getting the final volume of *Lyttelton* into shape.

Ever since Jonathan Bailey left Marrick Priory we had had great difficulty in finding an adequate successor. On 21 April we had a meeting in our house with the Bishop of Ripon in the chair, assisted by the Archdeacon, myself and Derek Dutton, the youthful headmaster of Richmond School, who had been a stalwart supporter of the Priory from the beginning. After a long discussion we persuaded the present warden to stay on until we had found a better man.

Some years ago a young man rang the front-door bell and asked whether we would like our windows cleaned. We said yes please – little knowing that he, Simon Hall, was to become our grass-cutter and every sort of handyman for many years. He became and still is one of the family.

Junie and I were doing most of the gardening together and were throughly enjoying it. Poor Nell had been ill for some time with an undiagnosed illness. Junie kept driving her to Scorton Hospital for treatment. She was already unable to do any work in the house.

On 18 May Diana Hood telephoned to say that Roger Fulford died peacefully during the night – my dear friend since Oxford in 1926. We drove to Barbon for his funeral. Henry Anglesey read the lesson beautifully.

For years now we had driven the Volvo, in which Junie's legs were too short to reach the pedals, and the Mini, into which I could only just fit. We were sad to part with the Volvo, in which I had driven 40,000 miles, but we decided to sell both cars and buy a Ford Fiesta, which we could both drive. When it arrived it was full of flowers.

Nell had been so ill that Junie had had to do all the housework for six weeks, as well as coping with visitors. We contacted Sister Christine at the Richmond Convent, who had told us that they

Pauline and Simon

employed a lot of women, each with her own car. Had she one who would do for us? As a result, on 27 June, Pauline Taylor, a pretty, smart, talkative widow of thirty came for coffee and arranged to come to us for two mornings a week, which was soon increased to three. With every year she has been more and more helpful, shopping for us and so on. She is happily still with us and we love her very much. After a few days she brought along George, a widower who knew about gardening. Willie was getting too old for it.

We were much cheered by an advance copy of *A Beggar in Purple*. Next day I recorded 'Did some weeding in rock garden with Pesky.'

Pauline, George and Simon came every Wednesday. On 1 September I wrote in my diary: 'We are so happy alone together that visitors, however nice, are an intrusion.' Nell was taken to North-allerton hospital, and her sister Jennie Fawcett drove Junie there to see her. Alas, Nell died on 11 September. Marske church was packed at her funeral: the clergyman gave out the wrong number of one of the hymns and was loudly corrected by the organist! This would have delighted Nell.

The proofs of *Lyttelton* VI began to arrive. On 11 November I wrote: 'A sodden foggy day which reminded me of exactly such weather on 11 November 1918.'

When I was shopping in Boots in December one of the prescription ladies ran after me and asked me whether I would inscribe a volume of Siegfried's war-diaries for her husband's Christmas present. This I graciously did.

It was fun to have four books published in 1983 – two Siegfrieds, *Lyttelton* V and *A Beggar in Purple*. Dear Eva Reichmann sent us her usual hamper of delicious food and drink for Christmas, and Reggie sent his usual six bottles of malt whisky.

[21]

January 1984 began with the usual snow, and one of our television aerials was blown off the roof. The snow was soon knee-deep, and one morning a herd of deer was seen in the village at first light. When the snow was a foot deep it was so firm that my 14 stone 8 didn't dent it. Pesky skidded about on it.

In February Junie took a large bouquet up to Willie and Martha to celebrate their golden wedding. The last of the tenants had mercifully left our cottage, and we all spent days clearing up rubbish and bringing filthy china and glasses back to our dish-washer. On 31 March Barbara Hodgson rented the tidy cottage and lived there for six years.

I was working on *More Letters of Oscar Wilde*, which Murray published in 1985. On 13 March (Hugh Walpole's hundredth birthday) I wrote an introduction to a new paperback edition of his *Portrait of a Man with Red Hair*.

On 15 April George Ramsden came and talked, clearly hoping to write my biography. I did not encourage or deter him. On 26 April the sixth and final *Lyttelton* volume was published. I was now correcting the proofs of Siegfried's 1923–5 diaries. For the next few weeks we were happily alone, gardening, reading proofs and books and watching television. It took us twenty-four hours to recover from visitors, however nice and dear.

Seeing no point in keeping the originals of the Lyttelton letters, so that tiresome students could find the few sentences which I had omitted to spare people's feelings, we burned the lot in our incinerator. I kept the first two for sentimental reasons.

Having been prevented by visitors from answering any letters, on one day I wrote twenty-three, and twenty postcards. New Oscar Wilde letters kept on arriving from my far-flung helpers, mostly in the USA.

On 13 June we received a case of champagne from my old friend Tony Powell, with a note saying that he had been awarded a large American literary prize and was sending presents to a few friends. I was a great admirer of his novels and had read the proofs of one or two for him. One he dedicated to me. It was appropriately titled *Books Do Furnish a Room*. I also received an unexpected cheque for £485 for a Japanese television version of a Hugh Walpole story.

At home in the library

On 22 June, after a long meeting at Marrick Priory, I announced my forthcoming retirement from the chairmanship of the committee, on which I had served since the first meeting to discuss the possibility of resurrecting the Priory.

In June Guy and Margaret Fisher came to stay, bringing with them a bottle of whisky, a box of chocolates, a new cricket book and a complete set of the R.H.-D. Ltd catalogues, which I was delighted to have.

In July David Sills our friend and solicitor came for a visit. We had never seen him before, but both liked him very much, and found him very intelligent and helpful.

A constant sentence in my diary reads 'Slept for nearly two hours after lunch, with Pesky warmly asleep on my lap.' It was Junie's sixtieth birthday on 9 August. She received seventeen cards and a lot of presents. I gave her a skirt, shirt and cardigan from the Scottish Woollen shop.

On 11 October there was a great luncheon party, twenty-five strong, at Marrick Priory to celebrate my retirement. The food was excellent, and there were speeches by Derek Dutton, the Archdeacon and me. I was given a lovely large water-colour picture of the Priory by Sam Chadwick, and Junie a large bunch of flowers. It was a happy occasion.

Marrick Priory by Sam Chadwick

On the same day I received a cheque for £2,300 for a Danish translation of Hugh's 'Herries Chronicles'. Junie bought a golden cushion for Pesky to sleep on, and she took to it at once. For three days running a wren came to the bird-table. We have never seen another one there.

George the gardener had a heart-attack and was taken to Catterick Hospital, where we visited him. He died a few days later.

On 12 December we heard that Junie had won £1,000 from Ernie. I spent a lot of time on *More Letters of Oscar Wilde*, assisted by many helpers: Owen Dudley Edwards, Ernest Mehew, Paul Chipchase, Henry Maas and a host of others. A peaceful end to the year.

[22]

As was customary, January 1985 produced plenty of snow, which made Pesky almost uncontrollably frisky. The oil-lorry got up to us at the third attempt, bringing enough oil to keep our heating going for a month. The north side of the house was a mass of long icicles.

Inspection of the rose garden by Pesky and me

June

The galley-proofs of *More Letters of Oscar Wilde* had gone to Murray and I was now working on the quite brief correspondence between Siegfried Sassoon and Max Beerbohm. One snowy day, as we sat down to lunch, five grouse flew into the back garden and sheltered under the bushes.

Siegfried's *1923–25 Diaries* were published on 7 March, and they got a good review by Tony Powell in the *Daily Telegraph*. My share of Lyttelton royalties in 1984 came to £1,332.

On April Fool's Day Pesky played a successful trick on us. She disappeared for several hours and we were very worried, until she was found snugly shut up in the airing cupboard. I corrected the page-proofs of *More Letters of Oscar Wilde* and compiled its index with Junie's

help. Jock Murray agreed to reprint the six Lyttelton volumes as three
paperback ones, two of the original volumes in each of three books.
This entailed our combining the indexes of six volumes, changing the
pagination in three of the volumes – a very tiring and tiresome job in
which Junie helped me as she always did in everything.

At the beginning of September we encountered a wonderfully
professional and courteous gesture from a shepherd. Driving home
along the top road we followed a large flock of sheep which were
blocking the road. Directly the shepherd saw us he sent his dog to the
front of the flock, and his whistles caused the dog to chase all the
sheep back behind our car, where the shepherd stopped them. One
doesn't often meet with such kind efficiency from busy shepherds.

Junie gave me a wonderful new toy, a kneeling-stool for 'senior
citizens' with firm handles for getting up and down, and just the thing
for my weeding.

A fearful gale in October blew eighty apples off our two Bramley
trees, leaving very few to be picked. In the same month I received a
cheque for £2,008 for my share of Ransome royalties.

On 11 December, after much X-raying I was operated on for
prostate at Scorton Hospital. Three days later, after a good deal of
pain, Junie drove me home. Alas, the operation was a failure.

A happy peaceful Christmas, when we were delighted to hear that
Pauline's seven-year-old daughter Christine put out a carrot for
Father Christmas's reindeer.

[23]

In January 1986 we finished the Lyttelton indexes, and I was very
glad to learn that in 1985 my books had earned £108 from the Public
Lending Rights Office. The bill for my failed prostate operation came
to £821.08 and BUPA paid it without a murmur. I longed to know
what the 08p was for.

I began to sort and arrange Max's letters for a volume of them.
Each March Junie brings in some twigs of forsythia, which quickly

come into flower. I was much cheered by a royalty cheque for £1,755 from John Murray.

I finished work on Siegfried Sassoon's letters to Max Beerbohm, with a few answers (thirty-nine from Siegfried and ten from Max). The book was published later in the year.

The heaviest snowfall we have known occurred that year. Jennie Fawcett's son Allan had to dig twenty-five pregnant ewes out of snowdrifts.

I have always enjoyed watching snooker on television, partly because it's the only game on television in which one can see *exactly* what's happening. The greatest and most enjoyable match was on 5 May 1986, when the 100–1 outsider Joe Johnson beat Steve Davis to become world champion.

On 18 July a male fan telephoned from Auckland, New Zealand, and June made friends and joked with him. I was very sad to read of Cuthbert Fitzherbert's death. He had been a great friend since 1941.

I spent a great deal of the summer watching Test Matches and other cricket on television. Botham was a great joy, fifty-nine in thirty-six balls and twenty-four in one over. Duff's children Guy and Alice came to stay.

With Alice, June and Guy

The whole roof of the house had to be replaced by a new one at hideous expense.

In September Duff and Phylla came for the night with a gentle Labrador called Zephyr, who, fiercely attacked by Pesky, fled in terror.

My diary for the rest of 1986 records:

> *21 October.* A bird-watcher's delight. The first things we saw were eight pheasants pecking about on the front lawn. At breakfast a host of jackdaws and a magpie descended on the back lawn. A wren and a nuthatch patronised the bird-table. Tits and chaffinches abounded. A Ransome royalty of £2,200 for the half-year.
>
> *26 November.* My mother's hundredth birthday, and she was only just forty when she died.
>
> *29 November.* Jonty Russell and his girl-friend Jo turned up. Jonty as charming and affectionate as ever.

[24]

The usual snow and icy temperatures marked the beginning of 1987. A royalty cheque for £1,176 came from John Murray. I was still collecting Max Beerbohm's letters from all over the world.

Bridget's daughter Amy came to stay, having intelligently discovered that the return coach-fare from London to Darlington was £12, whereas the train fare was £68. She is a dear girl and a perfect guest, always happy with a jigsaw puzzle.

Peter Barkworth gave a superb Siegfried Sassoon performance in the Georgian Theatre. He came to lunch the next day and we talked a lot about SS. On 3 June dear Jennie Fawcett, Nell's sister, died. She was our closest friend in the village, and in the Post Office she was the hub and centre of the whole place. For her funeral the village church was packed to overflowing with people standing.

> *30 June.* I weeded with Pesky in attendance. Charlie the damaged pheasant kept turning up for more food, and Junie had to ward off a flock of jackdaws so that he could eat it.

29 July. Reggie rang up to say Hugh Wheeler had died. Very sad. He was a dear fellow.

14 August. Old Willie (eighty-three) came down thinking it was my birthday and bringing chocolates, a handkerchief, a card and a lot of biscuits made by his wife Martha. He then fixed the clock in the drawing-room, which I had asked him to mend two years ago. He was a dear old man.

28 August. My eightieth birthday was a happy one. Fifty-seven cards and a mass of presents. Junie gave me a lovely standing book-rest, which she had had specially made. Adam gave me a pipe and a great deal of tobacco. Some of the family couldn't get here on the day, so a huge family gathering was arranged for 12 September, when we sat down fourteen including Pauline for supper.

3 November. Charlie the pheasant had been coming to us for food since June. When Junie got up she saw him fighting with another

My eightieth birthday party

cock pheasant. She put on woollies and wellies over her nightie and rushed out. When she reached the bottom of the front lawn the intruder flew off with a screech, and Charlie came up for grub.

7 November.   Helped Junie plant the Kilmarnock Willow in the round bed on the back lawn. Four bottles of Australian wine arrived from a female fan in New South Wales.

December.   Bobbie and Ivy brought their usual Christmas cake. He is eighty-one, she eighty, and they are as dear as ever. A happy Christmas day by ourselves.

[25]

The fierce snowy opening of 1988 kept away any visitors, and gave me time to correct the proofs of a volume of Max Beerbohm's letters. In April we were very cheered by a large Ransome royalty cheque.

I was re-reading one Trollope novel after another with great pleasure. The old boy knew how to hold one's attention, and I began roughing out my autobiographical book which was finally called *The Power of Chance*.

25 May.   Very sad to learn that Jamie Hamilton was dead.

13 June.   I bought a pretty little milk-jug for Junie on our twentieth (china) wedding anniversary. I started re-reading all the Sherlock Holmes volumes; the earliest are the best.

22 June.   Did a little path-clearing with Pesky.

17 September.   A man from Auckland, New Zealand, telephoned to say he had just been reading my *Hugh Walpole* and admired me very much. An encouraging start to the day.

29 September.   Pauline brought her Keith for the first time. He did a lot of work outside. Clearly a wonderful worker. We liked him very much. Dear Eva's Christmas present this year consisted of thirty-seven articles of food and drink.

[26]

January 1989 started with a bit of wild life in the back garden. A sparrowhawk swooped down, killed a blue tit and ate it on a branch of the fallen apple tree.

On 14 February we discovered almost half of our greenhouse reduced to smithereens by the previous night's gale. There was broken glass everywhere, which Junie and Pauline collected. We found that a new greenhouse would be terribly expensive, but after some discussion we decided to go ahead.

Two representatives of Sotheby's came and valued our pictures and furniture.

A Canadian couple rang the front door bell and told Junie they had come to Swaledale because they so much admired my books. Junie kindly told them I wasn't too well and they left.

The builder came and painted the woodwork of the new greenhouse without disturbing the sitting thrush.

Pesky here and there

On 13 June, our twenty-first wedding anniversary, Junie gave me a lovely thin summer jacket she had had specially made for me, and I have happily worn it every summer since.

From 4 August till 29 September we were terribly worried about Pesky's health. She wouldn't eat much and was clearly ill in some way. We took her several times to the vet in Richmond, who gave us all the remedies he thought might cure her. He took out several of her back teeth, which did her no good. She wanted to eat little. She stayed mostly out of doors. On 11 September I sat in the rocking-chair from 3.30 till 4.30 with Pesky on my lap, purring, scrabbling and sleeping: a very happy hour. But she was looking very thin and miserable, and on 29 September we took her to the vet for the last time. He told us that there was no hope of a cure, that she would inevitably get more pain and convulsions, so he had to end her life, and we drove home bereft and weeping; trying to cheer ourselves by saying that, except for the last eight weeks, she must have been the happiest and most loved cat in the world. For a long time we were both miserably unhappy, missing Pesky every moment. The rest of 1989 was a grey area to us. And nine years later we still miss her.

[27]

In February 1990 Barbara left the cottage, where she had lived for six years. We agreed to buy her fridge and washing machine, and as soon as she was gone Junie, our able neighbour David Noble and an army of workers began to improve and modernise the whole cottage into a cosy little home with three bedrooms, two bathrooms and two sitting-rooms facing south.

The village post-office in Marske had closed down, and we had to drive five miles to Reeth to get our pensions, for now shopping in Richmond was hideous with cars, parking and visitors.

I was working hard at my new autobiographical book, *The Power of Chance*, which was published in 1991.

The old man at work

One day in December Junie was driving home from Richmond when a young deer leaped over the hedge and dashed across the road, just missing the front of the car.

[28]

We had a wonderfully peaceful year in 1991, chiefly owing to Junie's miraculous tact on the telephone. During the year only seven visitors slept in this house, and four of them were family. We still had to collect our pensions from Reeth post-office, where dear Mrs Ellerton used to give us three or four weeks'-worth at once, to save us so many journeys in the winter snow. We were sad when we learned that she was retiring in June. Simon was busy decorating the inside of the cottage.

The persistent one-legged pheasant Charlie turned up with only one eye, and ate greedily as June fed him. We did as much shopping as possible in Reeth, which was only five miles away and there was never any difficulty in parking the car. But during the year both the butcher and one of the grocers shut up shop.

In April I made a start on this very book, and it's hard to believe how long it has taken me to write. I received a cheque for £700 of Walpole royalties, which I thought were the last to come, since his copyright expired in this year, fifty years after his death.[1]

On 14 June I was very sad to hear that my first wife Peg had died after three weeks of coma. We had always stayed affectionate friends, and she came several times to the Old Rectory.

We both worked hard at the index of *The Power of Chance*, which was published on 30 August and received good reviews, especially one by Philip Ziegler, whose wonderful review of the first Lyttelton volume set the whole of that series into action.

In that month I one day failed to get out of my bath, and June had to call in David Noble to pull me out. The same thing happened in November.

My eighty-fourth birthday was a happy one, with a mass of cards and presents. Duff sent us a mobile telephone, which has been a blessing ever since.

At the end of the year we watched the first part of Adam's television series, *Local Heroes*.

[29]

New Year's Day 1992 began with a gale-force wind, which knocked out half the dale's electricity. We made good with a coal-fire in the sitting-room and a calor-gas heater in the kitchen. After lunch the

---

[1] But now the copyrights of authors are valid for seventy instead of fifty years.

With Adam

power came on again. We were at last able to get our pensions from Val Simpson in her tiny village post-office, thus saving us drives to Reeth.

On 8 May we enjoyed watching the Middlesex Rugby Sevens, which were won by Western Samoa.

In June a new blessing came into our lives. Steve, the travelling fishmonger, lives at Grimsby, goes down to the docks there at 4.30 a.m. and buys every kind of fresh fish for his refrigerated van. He comes to us every Tuesday and what amuses us is the fact that he detests fish.

My eighty-fifth birthday on 28 August was a very happy day. Adam came for lunch, bringing eight kinds of rare tobaccos, a pipe, and a bottle of Moët et Chandon champagne, which we polished off before lunch.

We had long been looking for a local accountant, to avoid everything having to go to London and back, and then Simon and David Noble advised us to go to Tony Fava in Richmond, which we did: we like him very much. He and his highly efficient assistant Nina deal with all our affairs promptly and well.

At the beginning of the year I had firmly decided to spend an hour each day on this book, but alas I dawdled, and by the end of the year I had reached only 1949.

I had a pain in my right knee, which turned out to be arthritis. Dr Heron advised us to go to the specialist Dr Fordham at the Middlesbrough South Hospital. We drove over there. A few days later I became a patient in the Hospital of St John of God at Scorton. Dr Fordham came and gave me a cortisone injection in my knee, and four days later, after some simple treatment, I returned home with no pain. The bill for my four days in hospital and two sights of the specialist came to more than £1,000, which BUPA obligingly paid.

I was now slightly unsteady in my walking, and our splendid neighbour David Noble fixed a second banister on the main staircase, and hand-holds wherever in the house there are steps.

[30]

On the afternoon of 2 February 1993 I was asleep in the library, Junie on her bed reading. At 3 p.m. a burglar smashed half the French window in the drawing-room and stole all our little objects, including my christening mug and my Cooper grandfather's prize clock. Luckily, hearing a bit of a noise, Junie scrambled to her feet and the burglar ran for it. We immediately rang the police, who sent round two nice young constables, two CID men and a fingerprint expert, all to no avail.

Two days later I went down with influenza and was in bed for eight days. At the end of the month Dr Heron said I had shingles and prescribed a seven-day course of blue pills. On 19 March Junie drove us to Reeth, where we were warmly greeted by our friends in the shops: it was the first time for a month that I had been further than the garden.

On 1 April we were very sad to hear that dear Reggie Grenfell had died. Later we learned that he had left us £6,000 in his will, bless him.

Our Silver Wedding day was on 13 June. I gave Junie a pretty little table for her bedroom. Split a half-bottle of champagne in the evening of a happy day.

On the very next day I suffered a severe chest pain. Dr Kipling came and said I'd had a minor heart-attack. He summoned an ambulance which took me to the Friarage Hospital in Northallerton. He must have given me some sort of sedative because I had no recollection of the ambulance or of the intensive care ward in which I spent two days. When I came to I was in a little room of my own, with a WC and washbasin attached to it. There I was visited by Dr Somasundram, the great heart-specialist from Sri Lanka, a tall handsome man, smartly dressed and with a delicious sense of humour. I was twelve days in the hospital, and was delighted to be home again. Junie came to fetch me, and as we were at the door of the building two of the nurses ran up to give me farewell kisses.

In July we were sad to hear of Jock Murray's death.

In August Dr Somasundram came with his electrocardiac machine, with which he listened to my heart and then took my blood-pressure. He had a cup of tea with us, and when he got up to go I said, 'Dr Somasundram, you're not only a damn good doctor, but you're also a very nice kind man.' He turned to Junie and said, 'I'm blushing, I'm going a darker shade of brown.'

Junie suddenly had a very bad pain in the lower part of her spine. It was the first time in the twenty-eight years of our marriage that she had had more than a cold in the head. The doctor sent her to a physiotherapist, who pummelled her so hard that the pain increased. She was taken to Scorton Hospital for X-rays, Richmond for blood-tests, and later to Northallerton where Dr Walton gave her a little electric machine to fix in the small of her back. The pain lasted for months, and every few days our next-door neighbour Jill Hodge, who is a master cook, brought some delicious dishes which she made for us both. As I wrote in my diary: 'Junie is very brave and good and dear.'

Meanwhile Bridget's very belated but gratefully accepted birthday present arrived. It was a mechanical machine for the bath, which lifts one up and down.

One day in November two smiling young people rang the front door bell and asked me what I thought of the Bible. I told them that the Authorised Version was one of the great works in English literature, full of poetry and good prose, whereas the New English Bible was as dull as ditchwater. I said I was busy and they went smiling away.

On 26 November I noted 'Junie's best day since her pain began', and on 12 December she slept for an hour after lunch, her first such sleep for three months.

On 18 December dear old Willie's wife Martha died and Willie went to live with one of their daughters. On Christmas Eve Jill and her daughter Sarah brought us six different kinds of home-made delicacies. On the same day my persistent fan in Auckland, New Zealand, telephoned to say he loved all my books and wished me a happy Christmas.

Snow fell at the end of the year and I recorded: 'A cold day to end the year, in which I have endured osteo-arthritis, flu, shingles and a mild heart-attack. Junie's back is ever so much better and she is her darling self again.'

[31]

There is little to record in the next two years, since we never drove more than five miles to Richmond or Reeth unless we had to take a taxi to a doctor or hospital, and the vast company of visitors staying in the house was cut down to members of our families.

I enjoyed watching the Test Matches on television and was delighted to see the New Zealand side contained one man called Hart and another called Davis.

Junie's seventieth birthday was 9 August 1994 – lots of cards and presents, to which all our friends in the village contributed. Junie was overwhelmed. A week later I received a cheque for £50 from a Premium Bond I bought twenty-five years before.

My eighty-seventh birthday was a happy one, alone with Junie and a lot of cards and presents.

In December Junie and other friends went to see Willie on his ninetieth birthday. A few months later Junie went for the last time to see him, just before he died, and his last words to her, bless him, were 'How is Sir Rupert? Can he still get his socks on?' A very shrewd question.

On the last day of 1994 Deirdre's granddaughter Polly rang up to say that Deirdre's husband William had suddenly died without any illness. For sixteen years he had tenderly been looking after D in every way, and she will be desolate without him.

[32]

On 24 February 1995 Alice's charming husband Matthew rang up to say that she had given birth to an eight-pound baby girl, who was to be called Molly. My first great-grandchild, a tremendous thrill.

In March Pauline produced a first-rate gardener called Jim Lawson. We both took a great liking to him, and we were soon able to admire his spendid work.

On the snowy morning of 18 April Alice and Matthew brought baby Molly to see us. We were both entranced by her and were photographed holding her. Two years later her sister Beth was born. Later still Michèle, the wife of Adam's son Jason, produced my first great-grandson whom they are christening Louis Sewavi Rupert.

In June came our twenty-seventh wedding anniversary and in August my eighty-eighth birthday. In the same month we bought a

Molly, the first great-granddaughter

Beth, the second

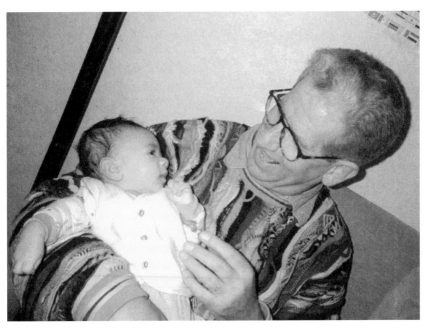

Louis Sewavi Rupert Hart-Davis with his grandfather

new Ford Fiesta car, and Bridget's Simon drove 500 miles to teach Junie how to handle it – a wonderful piece of good nature.

In September Dr Somasundram came to listen to my heart and take my blood-pressure. He said both were okay. He had a cup of tea and was his usual amusing self.

Now we come to 1996, fifty years after the first chapter of this book, and since I have now reached what Rupert Brooke called 'that unhoped serene that men call age', in my ninetieth year, halfway to Heaven, I think it's time to lay aside my pen and say farewell, not to Othello's occupation, but to my literary life.

APPENDIX A

Congratulations, best of men,
On having reached four score and ten,
And even more, the truth to tell,
On having used those years so well.
The shades of Oscar, Max and Hugh
And Reggie Turner, Siegfried too,
George Lyttelton and Arthur Ransome
Must bless your name, you've done 'em handsome.
And this is just to give you credit
For those you found the time to edit.
The place of honour on the shelf
Is for the books you wrote yourself.
We also recollect with praise
Those distant and exciting days
Publishing in Connaught Street
(With 'shaving accidents' to eat)
And later on in Soho Square
(With rather more distinguished fare),
Beginning with a slender book
On art and politics by Brooke,
The first of many works by James,
Then Potter's little book on Games-
manship (and Life-, One-Up- and Super-)
Three volumes of Diana Cooper,
Important series, such as those
Called Reynards, Mariners, Sohos,
Uncle Duff's *Old Men Forget,*

Le Hibou et la Poussiquette,
Books on cricket, submarines
And endless cousins of the Queen's,
On elephants, Tibet and figs,
Theosophy and keeping pigs,
On Blake and Yeats and Philip Sidney,
And other poets of that kidney,
Some novels on Accursed Kings
And very many other things.

Enough of that! Let's turn our view
To other things you used to do:
The Lit. Soc, and especially
The good old London Library,
And then, at Marske a little later,
The Richmond Georgian The-ay-ter.

But most of all we thank you dearly
For being Rupert,

                          yours sincerely,
                          Richard

PS We hope to see you soon,
With lots of love to you and June.

APPENDIX B

BOOKS DEDICATED TO RUPERT HART-DAVIS

1936 H.E. Bates *A House of Women*
1936 Edmund Blunden *Keats's Publisher*
1939 C. Day Lewis *Child of Misfortune* With Comfort
1944 J. Maclaren Ross *The Stuff to Give the Troops.*
1958 R.S. Thomas *Poetry for Supper* With John Betjeman
1959 Peter Fleming *The Siege at Peking*
1959 Ray Bradbury *The Day it Rained Forever*
1960 Diana Cooper *Trumpets from the Steep* With others
1962 Kenneth Hopkins *Body Blow*
1963 Eric Linklater *A Man Over Forty*
1966 Brian Hill *The Greedy Book* With Ruth
1968 Compton Mackenzie *Robert Louis Stevenson* With Ruth
1971 Anthony Powell *Books Do Furnish a Room*
1978 William Plomer *Electric Delights*
1983 Dan H. Laurence *Bibliography of Bernard Shaw* With June
1984 Leon Edel *Writing Lives*
1987 Hugh Brogan *Mowgli's Sons* With June
1988 Owen Dudley Edwards *Macaulay*
1990 J.G.P. Delany *Charles Ricketts: a Biography*
1994 J.G. Riewald *Collected Verse* by Max Beerbohm
1994 Guy Hart-Davis *Falcon 3*
1998 Adam Hart-Davis *Amazing Math Puzzles*

INDEX